Name _____ Date _____ Class _____

1-1 WORK TOGETHER, p. 11

Performing file maintenance activities; adding general ledger accounts

2120	Federal Income Tax Payable
2125	Social Security Tax Payable
	Medicare Tax Payable
	Unemployment Tax Payable—Federal
2130	Unemployment Tax Payable—State

1-1 ON YOUR OWN, p. 11

Performing file maintenance activities; adding general ledger accounts [5]

6205	Depreciation Expense—Office Equipment
	Payroll Taxes Expense
6210	Rent Expense
	Salary Expense—Administrative
6215	Supplies Expense—Office
	Utilities Expense

1-1 WORK TOGETHER

Extra form

1-2 WORK TOGETHER
ON YOUR OWN, p. 19

Journalizing and posting purchases on account and purchases returns and allowances [3, 5]

PURCHASES JOURNAL
PAGE 3

	DATE	ACCOUNT CREDITED	PURCH. NO.	POST. REF.	ACCOUNTS PAYABLE CREDIT	PURCHASES DEBIT	
						COMPACT DISCS	TAPES
1							
2							
3							
4							
5							
6							
7							
8							
9							
10							
11							

[3, 5]

PURCHASES RETURNS AND ALLOWANCES JOURNAL
PAGE 3

	DATE	ACCOUNT DEBITED	DEBIT MEMO. NO.	POST. REF.	ACCOUNTS PAYABLE DEBIT	PURCHASES RETURNS AND ALLOWANCES CREDIT	
						COMPACT DISCS	TAPES
1							
2							
3							
4							
5							
6							
7							
8							
9							
10							
11							
12							
13							
14							
15							

1-2 WORK TOGETHER
ON YOUR OWN (continued)

[4, 6]

GENERAL LEDGER

ACCOUNT Accounts Payable   ACCOUNT NO. 2105

DATE	ITEM	POST. REF.	DEBIT	CREDIT	BALANCE DEBIT	BALANCE CREDIT
20-- Mar. 1	Balance	✓				2 1 7 0 00

ACCOUNT Purchases—Compact Discs   ACCOUNT NO. 5105-1

DATE	ITEM	POST. REF.	DEBIT	CREDIT	BALANCE DEBIT	BALANCE CREDIT

ACCOUNT Purchases—Tapes   ACCOUNT NO. 5105-2

DATE	ITEM	POST. REF.	DEBIT	CREDIT	BALANCE DEBIT	BALANCE CREDIT

ACCOUNT Purchases Returns and Allowances—Compact Discs   ACCOUNT NO. 5110-1

DATE	ITEM	POST. REF.	DEBIT	CREDIT	BALANCE DEBIT	BALANCE CREDIT

ACCOUNT Purchases Returns and Allowances—Tapes   ACCOUNT NO. 5110-2

DATE	ITEM	POST. REF.	DEBIT	CREDIT	BALANCE DEBIT	BALANCE CREDIT

Name _____ Date _____ Class _____

1-2 WORK TOGETHER
ON YOUR OWN (continued)

[4, 6]

ACCOUNTS PAYABLE LEDGER

VENDOR Artex Music   **VENDOR NO.** 210

DATE		ITEM	POST. REF.	DEBIT	CREDIT	CREDIT BALANCE
20-- Mar.	1	Balance	✓			480 00

VENDOR Castle Records and Tapes   **VENDOR NO.** 220

DATE		ITEM	POST. REF.	DEBIT	CREDIT	CREDIT BALANCE
20-- Mar.	1	Balance	✓			760 00

VENDOR Dade, Inc.   **VENDOR NO.** 230

DATE		ITEM	POST. REF.	DEBIT	CREDIT	CREDIT BALANCE
20-- Mar.	1	Balance	✓			570 00

VENDOR Park Recording Company   **VENDOR NO.** 260

DATE		ITEM	POST. REF.	DEBIT	CREDIT	CREDIT BALANCE
20-- Mar.	1	Balance	✓			360 00

1-2 WORK TOGETHER / ON YOUR OWN (concluded)

[4, 6]

ACCOUNTS PAYABLE LEDGER

VENDOR Quality Tapes   VENDOR NO. 270

DATE	ITEM	POST. REF.	DEBIT	CREDIT	CREDIT BALANCE

VENDOR Raymond Wholesalers   VENDOR NO. 280

DATE	ITEM	POST. REF.	DEBIT	CREDIT	CREDIT BALANCE

Extra forms

VENDOR   VENDOR NO.

DATE	ITEM	POST. REF.	DEBIT	CREDIT	CREDIT BALANCE

VENDOR   VENDOR NO.

DATE	ITEM	POST. REF.	DEBIT	CREDIT	CREDIT BALANCE

1-3 WORK TOGETHER
ON YOUR OWN, p. 27

Journalizing and posting departmental cash payments [4, 6]

CASH PAYMENTS JOURNAL   PAGE 17

DATE	ACCOUNT TITLE	CK. NO.	POST. REF.	GENERAL DEBIT	GENERAL CREDIT	ACCOUNTS PAYABLE DEBIT	PURCH. DISCOUNT CR. GUITARS	PURCH. DISCOUNT CR. KEYBOARDS	CASH CREDIT

1-3 WORK TOGETHER
ON YOUR OWN (continued)

[5, 7]

GENERAL LEDGER

ACCOUNT Cash   **ACCOUNT NO.** 1105

DATE	ITEM	POST. REF.	DEBIT	CREDIT	BALANCE DEBIT	BALANCE CREDIT
20-- Sept. 1	Balance	✓			23 1 2 0 00	

ACCOUNT Petty Cash   **ACCOUNT NO.** 1110

DATE	ITEM	POST. REF.	DEBIT	CREDIT	BALANCE DEBIT	BALANCE CREDIT
20-- Sept. 1	Balance	✓			3 0 0 00	

ACCOUNT Supplies   **ACCOUNT NO.** 1130

DATE	ITEM	POST. REF.	DEBIT	CREDIT	BALANCE DEBIT	BALANCE CREDIT
20-- Sept. 1	Balance	✓			2 5 6 0 00	

ACCOUNT Accounts Payable   **ACCOUNT NO.** 2105

DATE	ITEM	POST. REF.	DEBIT	CREDIT	BALANCE DEBIT	BALANCE CREDIT
20-- Sept. 1	Balance	✓				1 9 6 3 00

1-3 WORK TOGETHER
ON YOUR OWN (continued)

[5, 7]

GENERAL LEDGER

ACCOUNT Purchases Discount—Guitars · ACCOUNT NO. 5115-1

DATE	ITEM	POST. REF.	DEBIT	CREDIT	BALANCE DEBIT	BALANCE CREDIT

ACCOUNT Purchases Discount—Keyboards · ACCOUNT NO. 5115-2

DATE	ITEM	POST. REF.	DEBIT	CREDIT	BALANCE DEBIT	BALANCE CREDIT

ACCOUNT Advertising Expense · ACCOUNT NO. 6105

DATE	ITEM	POST. REF.	DEBIT	CREDIT	BALANCE DEBIT	BALANCE CREDIT

ACCOUNT Credit Card Fee Expense · ACCOUNT NO. 6110

DATE	ITEM	POST. REF.	DEBIT	CREDIT	BALANCE DEBIT	BALANCE CREDIT

1-3 WORK TOGETHER
ON YOUR OWN (concluded)

[5, 7]

ACCOUNT Miscellaneous Expense   **ACCOUNT NO.** 6220

DATE	ITEM	POST. REF.	DEBIT	CREDIT	BALANCE DEBIT	BALANCE CREDIT

ACCOUNTS PAYABLE LEDGER

VENDOR Carmel Music   **VENDOR NO.** 210

DATE	ITEM	POST. REF.	DEBIT	CREDIT	CREDIT BALANCE
20-- Sept. 1	Balance	✓			1963 00

VENDOR Magic Keyboards   **VENDOR NO.** 220

DATE	ITEM	POST. REF.	DEBIT	CREDIT	CREDIT BALANCE
20-- Sept. 2		P14		3800 00	3800 00

VENDOR Peninsula Guitar   **VENDOR NO.** 230

DATE	ITEM	POST. REF.	DEBIT	CREDIT	CREDIT BALANCE
20-- Sept. 2		P14		800 00	800 00
3		P14		2030 00	2830 00

1-1 APPLICATION PROBLEM, p. 29

Performing file maintenance activities; adding general ledger accounts

1110	Cash
	Petty Cash
1115	Accounts Receivable
	Allowance for Uncollectible Accounts
1120	Merchandise Inventory
	Supplies—Office
1125	Supplies—Store
	Prepaid Insurance

1-1 APPLICATION PROBLEM

Extra form

1-2 APPLICATION PROBLEM, p. 29

Journalizing and posting departmental purchases on account and purchases returns and allowances [1, 2]

PURCHASES JOURNAL — PAGE 11

DATE	ACCOUNT CREDITED	PURCH. NO.	POST. REF.	ACCOUNTS PAYABLE CREDIT	PURCHASES DEBIT	
					CELLULAR PHONES	PAGERS

[1, 3]

PURCHASES RETURNS AND ALLOWANCES JOURNAL — PAGE 3

DATE	ACCOUNT DEBITED	DEBIT MEMO. NO.	POST. REF.	ACCOUNTS PAYABLE DEBIT	PURCHASES RETURNS AND ALLOWANCES CREDIT	
					CELLULAR PHONES	PAGERS

Chapter 1 Recording Departmental Purchases and Cash Payments • 13

1-2 APPLICATION PROBLEM (continued)

[2, 3]

GENERAL LEDGER

ACCOUNT: Accounts Payable   ACCOUNT NO. 2105

DATE	ITEM	POST. REF.	DEBIT	CREDIT	BALANCE DEBIT	BALANCE CREDIT
20-- Oct. 1	Balance	✓				2635.00

ACCOUNT: Purchases—Cellular Phones   ACCOUNT NO. 5105-1

DATE	ITEM	POST. REF.	DEBIT	CREDIT	BALANCE DEBIT	BALANCE CREDIT

ACCOUNT: Purchases—Pagers   ACCOUNT NO. 5105-2

DATE	ITEM	POST. REF.	DEBIT	CREDIT	BALANCE DEBIT	BALANCE CREDIT

ACCOUNT: Purchases Returns and Allowances—Cellular Phones   ACCOUNT NO. 5110-1

DATE	ITEM	POST. REF.	DEBIT	CREDIT	BALANCE DEBIT	BALANCE CREDIT

ACCOUNT: Purchases Returns and Allowances—Pagers   ACCOUNT NO. 5110-2

DATE	ITEM	POST. REF.	DEBIT	CREDIT	BALANCE DEBIT	BALANCE CREDIT

1-2 APPLICATION PROBLEM (continued)

[2, 3]

ACCOUNTS PAYABLE LEDGER

VENDOR Car Phone Wholesalers   **VENDOR NO.** 210

DATE	ITEM	POST. REF.	DEBIT	CREDIT	CREDIT BALANCE
20-- Oct. 1	Balance	✓			650 00

VENDOR Cell Advantage, Inc.   **VENDOR NO.** 220

DATE	ITEM	POST. REF.	DEBIT	CREDIT	CREDIT BALANCE

VENDOR ComSystems   **VENDOR NO.** 230

DATE	ITEM	POST. REF.	DEBIT	CREDIT	CREDIT BALANCE
20-- Oct. 1	Balance	✓			430 00

VENDOR ExecuPhone   **VENDOR NO.** 240

DATE	ITEM	POST. REF.	DEBIT	CREDIT	CREDIT BALANCE

1-2 APPLICATION PROBLEM (concluded)

[2, 3]

ACCOUNTS PAYABLE LEDGER

VENDOR PageMax, Inc.   **VENDOR NO.** 250

DATE	ITEM	POST. REF.	DEBIT	CREDIT	CREDIT BALANCE

VENDOR Phone Solution   **VENDOR NO.** 260

DATE	ITEM	POST. REF.	DEBIT	CREDIT	CREDIT BALANCE
20-- Oct. 1	Balance	✓			850 00

VENDOR Telecom Corporation   **VENDOR NO.** 270

DATE	ITEM	POST. REF.	DEBIT	CREDIT	CREDIT BALANCE

VENDOR Western Distributors   **VENDOR NO.** 280

DATE	ITEM	POST. REF.	DEBIT	CREDIT	CREDIT BALANCE
20-- Oct. 1	Balance	✓			705 00

1-3 APPLICATION PROBLEM, p. 30

Journalizing and posting departmental cash payments [1, 2]

CASH PAYMENTS JOURNAL — PAGE 21

DATE	ACCOUNT TITLE	CK. NO.	POST. REF.	GENERAL DEBIT	GENERAL CREDIT	ACCOUNTS PAYABLE DEBIT	PURCH. DISCOUNT CR. CRAFTS	PURCH. DISCOUNT CR. PLANTS	CASH CREDIT

1-3 APPLICATION PROBLEM (continued)

[1, 2]

GENERAL LEDGER

ACCOUNT Cash ACCOUNT NO. 1105

DATE		ITEM	POST. REF.	DEBIT	CREDIT	BALANCE DEBIT	BALANCE CREDIT
20-- Nov.	1	Balance	✓			18 380 00	

ACCOUNT Petty Cash ACCOUNT NO. 1110

DATE		ITEM	POST. REF.	DEBIT	CREDIT	BALANCE DEBIT	BALANCE CREDIT
20-- Nov.	1	Balance	✓			500 00	

ACCOUNT Supplies ACCOUNT NO. 1130

DATE		ITEM	POST. REF.	DEBIT	CREDIT	BALANCE DEBIT	BALANCE CREDIT
20-- Nov.	1	Balance	✓			1 260 00	

ACCOUNT Accounts Payable ACCOUNT NO. 2105

DATE		ITEM	POST. REF.	DEBIT	CREDIT	BALANCE DEBIT	BALANCE CREDIT
20-- Nov.	1	Balance	✓				885 00
	30		P11		5 513 00		6 398 00

ACCOUNT Purchases Discount—Crafts ACCOUNT NO. 5115-1

DATE	ITEM	POST. REF.	DEBIT	CREDIT	BALANCE DEBIT	BALANCE CREDIT

1-3 APPLICATION PROBLEM (continued)

[2]

GENERAL LEDGER

ACCOUNT Purchases Discount—Plants   ACCOUNT NO. 5115-2

DATE	ITEM	POST. REF.	DEBIT	CREDIT	BALANCE DEBIT	BALANCE CREDIT

ACCOUNT Advertising Expense   ACCOUNT NO. 6105

DATE	ITEM	POST. REF.	DEBIT	CREDIT	BALANCE DEBIT	BALANCE CREDIT

ACCOUNT Credit Card Fee Expense   ACCOUNT NO. 6110

DATE	ITEM	POST. REF.	DEBIT	CREDIT	BALANCE DEBIT	BALANCE CREDIT

ACCOUNT Miscellaneous Expense   ACCOUNT NO. 6220

DATE	ITEM	POST. REF.	DEBIT	CREDIT	BALANCE DEBIT	BALANCE CREDIT

ACCOUNT Rent Expense   ACCOUNT NO. 6230

DATE	ITEM	POST. REF.	DEBIT	CREDIT	BALANCE DEBIT	BALANCE CREDIT

1-3 APPLICATION PROBLEM (concluded)

[2]

ACCOUNTS PAYABLE LEDGER

VENDOR Century Crafts, Inc. **VENDOR NO.** 210

DATE	ITEM	POST. REF.	DEBIT	CREDIT	CREDIT BALANCE
20-- Nov. 6		P11		963 00	963 00

VENDOR Evergreen Trees & Shrubs **VENDOR NO.** 220

DATE	ITEM	POST. REF.	DEBIT	CREDIT	CREDIT BALANCE
20-- Nov. 16		P11		1840 00	1840 00
20		P11		1460 00	3300 00

VENDOR Northtown Plants **VENDOR NO.** 230

DATE	ITEM	POST. REF.	DEBIT	CREDIT	CREDIT BALANCE
20-- Nov. 3		P11		1250 00	1250 00

VENDOR Wholesale Crafts, Inc. **VENDOR NO.** 240

DATE	ITEM	POST. REF.	DEBIT	CREDIT	CREDIT BALANCE
20-- Nov. 1	Balance	✓			885 00

1-4 APPLICATION PROBLEM, p. 30

Reconciling a bank statement

RECONCILIATION OF BANK STATEMENT   Date _____

1. Enter CHECKBOOK BALANCE as shown on check stub.
2. Enter and add bank charges to obtain TOTAL BANK CHARGES.
3. Deduct TOTAL BANK CHARGES from CHECKBOOK BALANCE to obtain ADJUSTED CHECKBOOK BALANCE.
4. Enter BANK BALANCE as shown on bank statement.
5. Enter and add the amounts of any outstanding deposits recorded on the check stubs but not listed on the bank statement to obtain TOTAL OUTSTANDING DEPOSITS.
6. Add TOTAL OUTSTANDING DEPOSITS to BANK BALANCE to obtain TOTAL.
7. Sort all checks included in the statement numerically or by date issued.
   a. Check off on the check stubs of the checkbook each of the checks paid by the bank.
   b. Enter the check numbers and amounts of checks still outstanding.
   c. Add the outstanding checks to obtain TOTAL OUTSTANDING CHECKS.
8. Deduct TOTAL OUTSTANDING CHECKS from TOTAL to obtain ADJUSTED BANK BALANCE.
9. The ADJUSTED CHECKBOOK BALANCE and the ADJUSTED BANK BALANCE should agree, proving that both the checkbook balance and the bank balance are correct.

(1) CHECKBOOK BALANCE.............. $ _____   (4) BANK BALANCE........................ $ _____

BANK CHARGES

Description	Amount	
Service Charge		

OUTSTANDING DEPOSITS

Date	Amount	

(5) ADD TOTAL OUTSTANDING DEPOSITS................................. $ _____

(6) TOTAL................................... $ _____

OUTSTANDING CHECKS

CK. NO.	Amount	

(2) DEDUCT TOTAL BANK CHARGES.... $ _____

(7) DEDUCT TOTAL OUTSTANDING CHECKS................................. $ _____

(3) ADJUSTED CHECKBOOK BALANCE. $ _____   (8) ADJUSTED BANK BALANCE.......... $ _____

1-4 APPLICATION PROBLEM

Extra form

RECONCILIATION OF BANK STATEMENT   Date _____

1. Enter CHECKBOOK BALANCE as shown on check stub.
2. Enter and add bank charges to obtain TOTAL BANK CHARGES.
3. Deduct TOTAL BANK CHARGES from CHECKBOOK BALANCE to obtain ADJUSTED CHECKBOOK BALANCE.
4. Enter BANK BALANCE as shown on bank statement.
5. Enter and add the amounts of any outstanding deposits recorded on the check stubs but not listed on the bank statement to obtain TOTAL OUTSTANDING DEPOSITS.
6. Add TOTAL OUTSTANDING DEPOSITS to BANK BALANCE to obtain TOTAL.
7. Sort all checks included in the statement numerically or by date issued.
   a. Check off on the check stubs of the checkbook each of the checks paid by the bank.
   b. Enter the check numbers and amounts of checks still outstanding.
   c. Add the outstanding checks to obtain TOTAL OUTSTANDING CHECKS.
8. Deduct TOTAL OUTSTANDING CHECKS from TOTAL to obtain ADJUSTED BANK BALANCE.
9. The ADJUSTED CHECKBOOK BALANCE and the ADJUSTED BANK BALANCE should agree, proving that both the checkbook balance and the bank balance are correct.

(1) CHECKBOOK BALANCE................ $ _____   (4) BANK BALANCE........................ $ _____

BANK CHARGES

Description	Amount	
Service Charge		

OUTSTANDING DEPOSITS

Date	Amount	

(5) ADD TOTAL OUTSTANDING DEPOSITS................................. $ _____

(6) TOTAL.. $ _____

OUTSTANDING CHECKS

CK. NO.	Amount	

(2) DEDUCT TOTAL BANK CHARGES.... $ _____   (7) DEDUCT TOTAL OUTSTANDING CHECKS............................... $ _____

(3) ADJUSTED CHECKBOOK BALANCE. $ _____   (8) ADJUSTED BANK BALANCE.......... $ _____

1-5 MASTERY PROBLEM, p. 31

Performing file maintenance activities; journalizing departmental purchases and cash payments; reconciling a bank statement [1]

6205	Depreciation Expense—Office Equipment
	Insurance Expense
6210	Miscellaneous Expense
6215	Rent Expense
6220	Supplies Expense—Office
6225	Supplies Expense—Store
	Uncollectible Accounts Expense

[2, 5]

PURCHASES JOURNAL PAGE 11

	DATE	ACCOUNT CREDITED	PURCH. NO.	POST. REF.	ACCOUNTS PAYABLE CREDIT	PURCHASES DEBIT CAMERAS	PURCHASES DEBIT ACCESSORIES	
1								1
2								2
3								3
4								4
5								5
6								6
7								7
8								8
9								9
10								10

[2, 5]

PURCHASES RETURNS AND ALLOWANCES JOURNAL PAGE 11

	DATE	ACCOUNT DEBITED	DEBIT MEMO. NO.	POST. REF.	ACCOUNTS PAYABLE DEBIT	PURCHASES RETURNS AND ALLOWANCES CREDIT CAMERAS	PURCHASES RETURNS AND ALLOWANCES CREDIT ACCESSORIES	
1								1
2								2
3								3
4								4
5								5
6								6

1-5 MASTERY PROBLEM (continued)

[2, 4, 5]

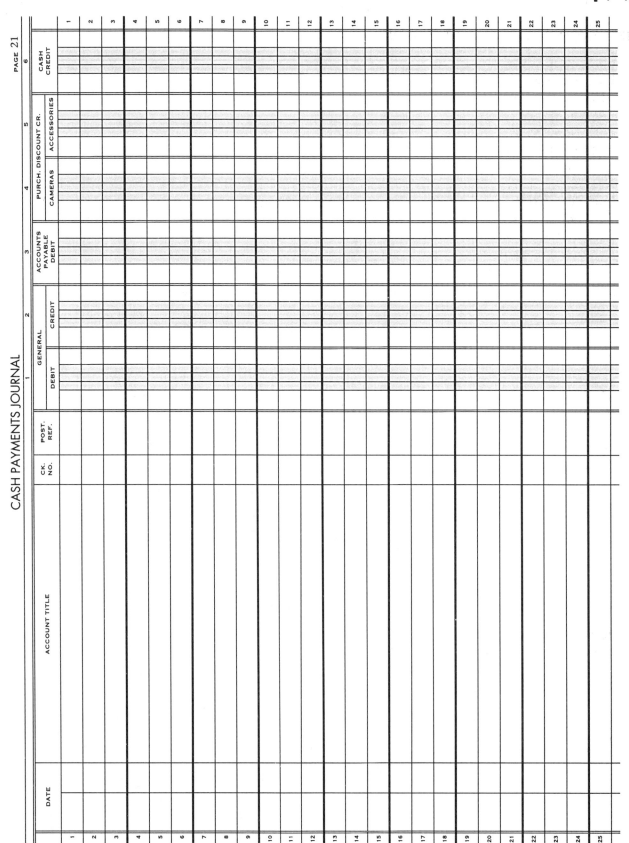

Name _____ Date _____ Class _____

1-5 MASTERY PROBLEM (concluded)

[3]

RECONCILIATION OF BANK STATEMENT Date _____

1. Enter CHECKBOOK BALANCE as shown on check stub.
2. Enter and add bank charges to obtain TOTAL BANK CHARGES.
3. Deduct TOTAL BANK CHARGES from CHECKBOOK BALANCE to obtain ADJUSTED CHECKBOOK BALANCE.
4. Enter BANK BALANCE as shown on bank statement.
5. Enter and add the amounts of any outstanding deposits recorded on the check stubs but not listed on the bank statement to obtain TOTAL OUTSTANDING DEPOSITS.
6. Add TOTAL OUTSTANDING DEPOSITS to BANK BALANCE to obtain TOTAL.
7. Sort all checks included in the statement numerically or by date issued.
   a. Check off on the check stubs of the checkbook each of the checks paid by the bank.
   b. Enter the check numbers and amounts of checks still outstanding.
   c. Add the outstanding checks to obtain TOTAL OUTSTANDING CHECKS.
8. Deduct TOTAL OUTSTANDING CHECKS from TOTAL to obtain ADJUSTED BANK BALANCE.
9. The ADJUSTED CHECKBOOK BALANCE and the ADJUSTED BANK BALANCE should agree, proving that both the checkbook balance and the bank balance are correct.

(1) CHECKBOOK BALANCE .... $ _____

BANK CHARGES

Description	Amount	
Service Charge		

(2) DEDUCT TOTAL BANK CHARGES .... $ _____

(3) ADJUSTED CHECKBOOK BALANCE . $ _____

(4) BANK BALANCE .... $ _____

OUTSTANDING DEPOSITS

Date	Amount	

(5) ADD TOTAL OUTSTANDING DEPOSITS .... $ _____

(6) TOTAL .... $ _____

OUTSTANDING CHECKS

CK. NO.	Amount	

(7) DEDUCT TOTAL OUTSTANDING CHECKS .... $ _____

(8) ADJUSTED BANK BALANCE .... $ _____

1-5 MASTERY PROBLEM

Extra form

RECONCILIATION OF BANK STATEMENT   Date _____

1. Enter CHECKBOOK BALANCE as shown on check stub.
2. Enter and add bank charges to obtain TOTAL BANK CHARGES.
3. Deduct TOTAL BANK CHARGES from CHECKBOOK BALANCE to obtain ADJUSTED CHECKBOOK BALANCE.
4. Enter BANK BALANCE as shown on bank statement.
5. Enter and add the amounts of any outstanding deposits recorded on the check stubs but not listed on the bank statement to obtain TOTAL OUTSTANDING DEPOSITS.
6. Add TOTAL OUTSTANDING DEPOSITS to BANK BALANCE to obtain TOTAL.
7. Sort all checks included in the statement numerically or by date issued.
   a. Check off on the check stubs of the checkbook each of the checks paid by the bank.
   b. Enter the check numbers and amounts of checks still outstanding.
   c. Add the outstanding checks to obtain TOTAL OUTSTANDING CHECKS.
8. Deduct TOTAL OUTSTANDING CHECKS from TOTAL to obtain ADJUSTED BANK BALANCE.
9. The ADJUSTED CHECKBOOK BALANCE and the ADJUSTED BANK BALANCE should agree, proving that both the checkbook balance and the bank balance are correct.

(1) CHECKBOOK BALANCE............. $ _____

BANK CHARGES

Description	Amount	
Service Charge		

(2) DEDUCT TOTAL BANK CHARGES.... $ _____

(3) ADJUSTED CHECKBOOK BALANCE. $ _____

(4) BANK BALANCE........................ $ _____

OUTSTANDING DEPOSITS

Date	Amount	

(5) ADD TOTAL OUTSTANDING DEPOSITS................................ $ _____

(6) TOTAL .... $ _____

OUTSTANDING CHECKS

CK. NO.	Amount	

(7) DEDUCT TOTAL OUTSTANDING CHECKS .... $ _____

(8) ADJUSTED BANK BALANCE.......... $ _____

1-6 CHALLENGE PROBLEM, p. 32

Journalizing purchases at net amount and using the account Discounts Lost [1, 2]

PURCHASES JOURNAL
PAGE 11

	DATE	ACCOUNT CREDITED	PURCH. NO.	POST. REF.	ACCOUNTS PAYABLE CREDIT (1)	PURCHASES DEBIT CAMERAS (2)	PURCHASES DEBIT ACCESSORIES (3)	
1								1
2								2
3								3
4								4
5								5
6								6
7								7
8								8
9								9
10								10
11								11

[1, 2]

PURCHASES RETURNS AND ALLOWANCES JOURNAL
PAGE 11

	DATE	ACCOUNT DEBITED	DEBIT MEMO. NO.	POST. REF.	ACCOUNTS PAYABLE DEBIT (1)	PURCHASES RETURNS AND ALLOWANCES CREDIT CAMERAS (2)	PURCHASES RETURNS AND ALLOWANCES CREDIT ACCESSORIES (3)	
1								1
2								2
3								3
4								4
5								5
6								6
7								7
8								8
9								9
10								10
11								11
12								12
13								13
14								14
15								15

1-6 CHALLENGE PROBLEM (concluded)

[1, 2]

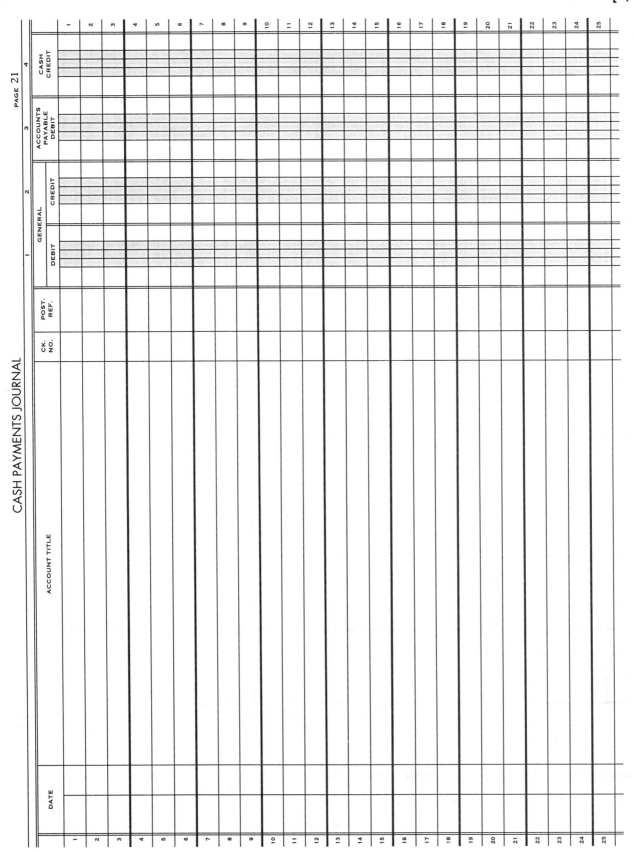

2-1 WORK TOGETHER
ON YOUR OWN, p. 47

Journalizing and posting departmental sales on account and sales returns and allowances [3-7]

SALES JOURNAL
PAGE 9

	DATE	ACCOUNT DEBITED	SALE NO.	POST. REF.	ACCOUNTS RECEIVABLE DEBIT (1)	SALES TAX PAYABLE CREDIT (2)	SALES CREDIT SWIMWEAR (3)	SALES CREDIT ACCESSORIES (4)	
1									1
2									2
3									3
4									4
5									5
6									6
7									7
8									8
9									9
10									10
11									11

SALES RETURNS AND ALLOWANCES JOURNAL
PAGE 9

	DATE	ACCOUNT CREDITED	CREDIT MEMO. NO.	POST. REF.	ACCOUNTS RECEIVABLE CREDIT (1)	SALES TAX PAYABLE DEBIT (2)	SALES RETURNS AND ALLOWANCES DEBIT SWIMWEAR (3)	SALES RETURNS AND ALLOWANCES DEBIT ACCESSORIES (4)	
1									1
2									2
3									3
4									4
5									5
6									6
7									7
8									8
9									9
10									10
11									11
12									12
13									13
14									14
15									15

2-1 WORK TOGETHER / ON YOUR OWN (continued)

[4, 6, 7]

GENERAL LEDGER

ACCOUNT: Accounts Receivable   ACCOUNT NO. 1115

DATE		ITEM	POST. REF.	DEBIT	CREDIT	BALANCE DEBIT	BALANCE CREDIT
20-- Sept.	1	Balance	✓			239 50	

ACCOUNT: Sales Tax Payable   ACCOUNT NO. 2130

DATE		ITEM	POST. REF.	DEBIT	CREDIT	BALANCE DEBIT	BALANCE CREDIT
20-- Sept.	1	Balance	✓				123 20

ACCOUNT: Sales—Swimwear   ACCOUNT NO. 4105-1

DATE	ITEM	POST. REF.	DEBIT	CREDIT	BALANCE DEBIT	BALANCE CREDIT

ACCOUNT: Sales—Accessories   ACCOUNT NO. 4105-2

DATE	ITEM	POST. REF.	DEBIT	CREDIT	BALANCE DEBIT	BALANCE CREDIT

ACCOUNT: Sales Returns and Allowances—Swimwear   ACCOUNT NO. 4110-1

DATE	ITEM	POST. REF.	DEBIT	CREDIT	BALANCE DEBIT	BALANCE CREDIT

ACCOUNT: Sales Returns and Allowances—Accessories   ACCOUNT NO. 4110-2

DATE	ITEM	POST. REF.	DEBIT	CREDIT	BALANCE DEBIT	BALANCE CREDIT

2-1 WORK TOGETHER, ON YOUR OWN (continued)

[4, 6, 7]

ACCOUNTS RECEIVABLE LEDGER

CUSTOMER Dana Brein   **CUSTOMER NO.** 110

DATE		ITEM	POST. REF.	DEBIT	CREDIT	DEBIT BALANCE
20-- Sept.	1	Balance	✓			5 5 00

CUSTOMER Kim Lockhart   **CUSTOMER NO.** 120

DATE		ITEM	POST. REF.	DEBIT	CREDIT	DEBIT BALANCE
20-- Sept.	1	Balance	✓			1 3 6 00

CUSTOMER John Muller   **CUSTOMER NO.** 130

DATE		ITEM	POST. REF.	DEBIT	CREDIT	DEBIT BALANCE
20-- Sept.	1	Balance	✓			4 8 50

CUSTOMER Western High School Swim Team   **CUSTOMER NO.** 140

DATE	ITEM	POST. REF.	DEBIT	CREDIT	DEBIT BALANCE

2-1 WORK TOGETHER / ON YOUR OWN

Extra forms

CUSTOMER _____ CUSTOMER NO. _____

DATE	ITEM	POST. REF.	DEBIT	CREDIT	DEBIT BALANCE

CUSTOMER _____ CUSTOMER NO. _____

DATE	ITEM	POST. REF.	DEBIT	CREDIT	DEBIT BALANCE

CUSTOMER _____ CUSTOMER NO. _____

DATE	ITEM	POST. REF.	DEBIT	CREDIT	DEBIT BALANCE

CUSTOMER _____ CUSTOMER NO. _____

DATE	ITEM	POST. REF.	DEBIT	CREDIT	DEBIT BALANCE

CUSTOMER _____ CUSTOMER NO. _____

DATE	ITEM	POST. REF.	DEBIT	CREDIT	DEBIT BALANCE

2-2 WORK TOGETHER / ON YOUR OWN, p. 54

Journalizing and posting departmental cash receipts [3, 5, 7]

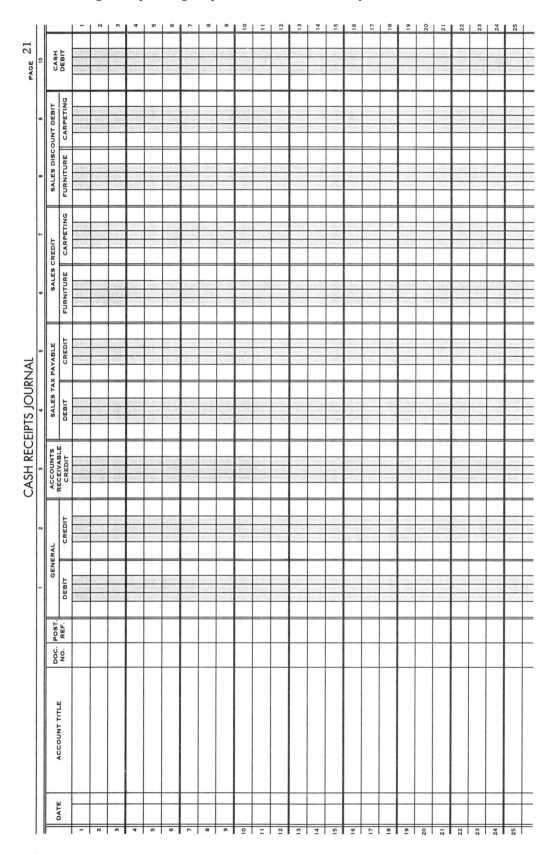

2-2 WORK TOGETHER / ON YOUR OWN (continued)

[4, 6, 7]

GENERAL LEDGER

ACCOUNT Cash   ACCOUNT NO. 1105

DATE		ITEM	POST. REF.	DEBIT	CREDIT	BALANCE DEBIT	BALANCE CREDIT
20-- Feb.	1	Balance	✓			43 3 4 0 00	

ACCOUNT Accounts Receivable   ACCOUNT NO. 1115

DATE		ITEM	POST. REF.	DEBIT	CREDIT	BALANCE DEBIT	BALANCE CREDIT
20-- Feb.	1	Balance	✓			4 1 1 8 10	

ACCOUNT Sales Tax Payable   ACCOUNT NO. 2130

DATE		ITEM	POST. REF.	DEBIT	CREDIT	BALANCE DEBIT	BALANCE CREDIT
20-- Feb.	1	Balance	✓				3 8 7 0 00

ACCOUNT Sales—Furniture   ACCOUNT NO. 4105-1

DATE	ITEM	POST. REF.	DEBIT	CREDIT	BALANCE DEBIT	BALANCE CREDIT

Name _____ Date _____ Class _____

2-2 WORK TOGETHER
ON YOUR OWN (continued)

[4, 6, 7]

GENERAL LEDGER

ACCOUNT Sales—Carpeting　　　　　　　　　　　　　　　　　　　ACCOUNT NO. 4105-2

DATE	ITEM	POST. REF.	DEBIT	CREDIT	BALANCE DEBIT	BALANCE CREDIT

ACCOUNT Sales Discount—Furniture　　　　　　　　　　　　　　　ACCOUNT NO. 4115-1

DATE	ITEM	POST. REF.	DEBIT	CREDIT	BALANCE DEBIT	BALANCE CREDIT

ACCOUNT Sales Discount—Carpeting　　　　　　　　　　　　　　ACCOUNT NO. 4115-2

DATE	ITEM	POST. REF.	DEBIT	CREDIT	BALANCE DEBIT	BALANCE CREDIT

Extra form

ACCOUNT　　　　　　　　　　　　　　　　　　　　　　　　　　　ACCOUNT NO.

DATE	ITEM	POST. REF.	DEBIT	CREDIT	BALANCE DEBIT	BALANCE CREDIT

2-2 WORK TOGETHER / ON YOUR OWN (concluded)

[4, 6]

ACCOUNTS RECEIVABLE LEDGER

CUSTOMER Mona Andrews Design   CUSTOMER NO. 110

DATE		ITEM	POST. REF.	DEBIT	CREDIT	DEBIT BALANCE
20-- Feb.	1	Balance	✓			2 0 7 0 20

CUSTOMER Joan Seymour   CUSTOMER NO. 120

DATE		ITEM	POST. REF.	DEBIT	CREDIT	DEBIT BALANCE
20-- Feb.	1	Balance	✓			7 4 2 00

CUSTOMER Bob Smits   CUSTOMER NO. 130

DATE		ITEM	POST. REF.	DEBIT	CREDIT	DEBIT BALANCE
20-- Feb.	1	Balance	✓			8 5 3 20

Extra form

CUSTOMER   CUSTOMER NO.

DATE	ITEM	POST. REF.	DEBIT	CREDIT	DEBIT BALANCE

2-1 APPLICATION PROBLEM p. 56

Journalizing and posting departmental sales on account and sales returns and allowances [1, 2]

SALES JOURNAL — PAGE 4

DATE	ACCOUNT DEBITED	SALE NO.	POST. REF.	ACCOUNTS RECEIVABLE DEBIT	SALES TAX PAYABLE CREDIT	SALES CREDIT	
						CLOTHING	SHOES

[1, 3]

SALES RETURNS AND ALLOWANCES JOURNAL — PAGE 4

DATE	ACCOUNT CREDITED	CREDIT MEMO. NO.	POST. REF.	ACCOUNTS RECEIVABLE CREDIT	SALES TAX PAYABLE DEBIT	SALES RETURNS AND ALLOWANCES DEBIT	
						CLOTHING	SHOES

2-1 APPLICATION PROBLEM (continued)

[2, 3]

GENERAL LEDGER

ACCOUNT Accounts Receivable　　　　　　　　　　　　　　ACCOUNT NO. 1115

DATE	ITEM	POST. REF.	DEBIT	CREDIT	BALANCE DEBIT	BALANCE CREDIT
20-- Apr. 1	Balance	✓			1 5 5 8 75	

ACCOUNT Sales Tax Payable　　　　　　　　　　　　　　ACCOUNT NO. 2130

DATE	ITEM	POST. REF.	DEBIT	CREDIT	BALANCE DEBIT	BALANCE CREDIT
20-- Apr. 1	Balance	✓				1 5 8 70

ACCOUNT Sales—Clothing　　　　　　　　　　　　　　ACCOUNT NO. 4105-1

DATE	ITEM	POST. REF.	DEBIT	CREDIT	BALANCE DEBIT	BALANCE CREDIT

ACCOUNT Sales—Shoes　　　　　　　　　　　　　　ACCOUNT NO. 4105-2

DATE	ITEM	POST. REF.	DEBIT	CREDIT	BALANCE DEBIT	BALANCE CREDIT

ACCOUNT Sales Returns and Allowances—Clothing　　　　　　ACCOUNT NO. 4110-1

DATE	ITEM	POST. REF.	DEBIT	CREDIT	BALANCE DEBIT	BALANCE CREDIT

ACCOUNT Sales Returns and Allowances—Shoes　　　　　　ACCOUNT NO. 4110-2

DATE	ITEM	POST. REF.	DEBIT	CREDIT	BALANCE DEBIT	BALANCE CREDIT

2-1 APPLICATION PROBLEM (continued)

[1]

ACCOUNTS RECEIVABLE LEDGER

CUSTOMER Archibald School District   **CUSTOMER NO.** 110

DATE	ITEM	POST. REF.	DEBIT	CREDIT	DEBIT BALANCE
20-- Apr. 1	Balance	✓			325 00

CUSTOMER Dana Eggers   **CUSTOMER NO.** 120

DATE	ITEM	POST. REF.	DEBIT	CREDIT	DEBIT BALANCE
20-- Apr. 1	Balance	✓			472 50

CUSTOMER Cherie Grecki   **CUSTOMER NO.** 130

DATE	ITEM	POST. REF.	DEBIT	CREDIT	DEBIT BALANCE
20-- Apr. 1	Balance	✓			299 25

CUSTOMER Phil Kellerman   **CUSTOMER NO.** 140

DATE	ITEM	POST. REF.	DEBIT	CREDIT	DEBIT BALANCE

CUSTOMER Ben Nesbitt   **CUSTOMER NO.** 150

DATE	ITEM	POST. REF.	DEBIT	CREDIT	DEBIT BALANCE
20-- Apr. 1	Balance	✓			273 00

Name _____ Date _____ Class _____

2-1 APPLICATION PROBLEM (concluded)

[1]

ACCOUNTS RECEIVABLE LEDGER

CUSTOMER Debbie Prosser   CUSTOMER NO. 160

DATE	ITEM	POST. REF.	DEBIT	CREDIT	DEBIT BALANCE

CUSTOMER Carole Tate   CUSTOMER NO. 170

DATE		ITEM	POST. REF.	DEBIT	CREDIT	DEBIT BALANCE
20-- Apr.	1	Balance	✓			1 8 9 00

CUSTOMER Wade Thomas   CUSTOMER NO. 180

DATE	ITEM	POST. REF.	DEBIT	CREDIT	DEBIT BALANCE

Extra form

CUSTOMER   CUSTOMER NO.

DATE	ITEM	POST. REF.	DEBIT	CREDIT	DEBIT BALANCE

2-2 APPLICATION PROBLEM, p. 56

Journalizing and posting departmental cash receipts [1, 2]

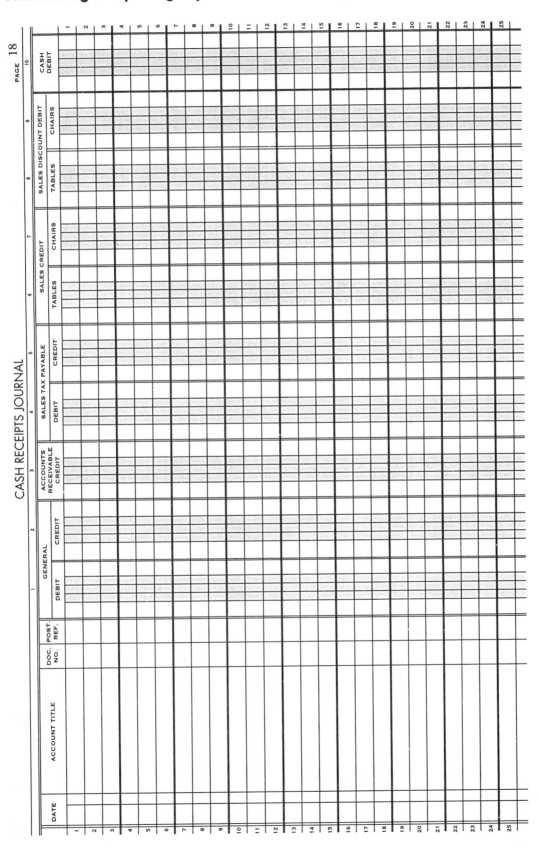

2-2 APPLICATION PROBLEM (continued)

[2]

GENERAL LEDGER

ACCOUNT Cash   ACCOUNT NO. 1105

DATE	ITEM	POST. REF.	DEBIT	CREDIT	BALANCE DEBIT	BALANCE CREDIT
20-- June 1	Balance	✓			59 913 00	

ACCOUNT Accounts Receivable   ACCOUNT NO. 1115

DATE	ITEM	POST. REF.	DEBIT	CREDIT	BALANCE DEBIT	BALANCE CREDIT
20-- June 1	Balance	✓			3 541 20	

ACCOUNT Sales Tax Payable   ACCOUNT NO. 2130

DATE	ITEM	POST. REF.	DEBIT	CREDIT	BALANCE DEBIT	BALANCE CREDIT
20-- June 1	Balance	✓				446 00

ACCOUNT Sales—Tables   ACCOUNT NO. 4105-1

DATE	ITEM	POST. REF.	DEBIT	CREDIT	BALANCE DEBIT	BALANCE CREDIT

ACCOUNT Sales—Chairs   ACCOUNT NO. 4105-2

DATE	ITEM	POST. REF.	DEBIT	CREDIT	BALANCE DEBIT	BALANCE CREDIT

2-2 APPLICATION PROBLEM (continued)

[1, 2]

GENERAL LEDGER

ACCOUNT Sales Discount—Tables ACCOUNT NO. 4115-1

DATE	ITEM	POST. REF.	DEBIT	CREDIT	BALANCE DEBIT	BALANCE CREDIT

ACCOUNT Sales Discount—Chairs ACCOUNT NO. 4115-2

DATE	ITEM	POST. REF.	DEBIT	CREDIT	BALANCE DEBIT	BALANCE CREDIT

ACCOUNTS RECEIVABLE LEDGER

CUSTOMER Amy Cannon CUSTOMER NO. 110

DATE	ITEM	POST. REF.	DEBIT	CREDIT	DEBIT BALANCE
20-- June 1	Balance	✓			823 70

CUSTOMER Wayne Miller CUSTOMER NO. 120

DATE	ITEM	POST. REF.	DEBIT	CREDIT	DEBIT BALANCE
20-- June 1	Balance	✓			200 00

2-2 APPLICATION PROBLEM (concluded)

[1]

ACCOUNTS RECEIVABLE LEDGER

CUSTOMER Joe Ricardo CUSTOMER NO. 130

DATE		ITEM	POST. REF.	DEBIT	CREDIT	DEBIT BALANCE
20-- June	1	Balance	✓			1059 90

CUSTOMER David Ring CUSTOMER NO. 140

DATE		ITEM	POST. REF.	DEBIT	CREDIT	DEBIT BALANCE
20-- June	1	Balance	✓			451 50

CUSTOMER Dawn Sanzone CUSTOMER NO. 150

DATE		ITEM	POST. REF.	DEBIT	CREDIT	DEBIT BALANCE
20-- June	1	Balance	✓			525 00

CUSTOMER Bob Witt CUSTOMER NO. 160

DATE		ITEM	POST. REF.	DEBIT	CREDIT	DEBIT BALANCE
20-- June	1	Balance	✓			481 10

2-3 MASTERY PROBLEM, p. 58

Journalizing departmental sales, sales returns and allowances, and cash receipts [1, 2]

SALES JOURNAL
PAGE 6

DATE	ACCOUNT DEBITED	SALE NO.	POST. REF.	ACCOUNTS RECEIVABLE DEBIT	SALES TAX PAYABLE CREDIT	SALES CREDIT — MEN'S CLOTHING	SALES CREDIT — WOMEN'S CLOTHING

[1, 2]

SALES RETURNS AND ALLOWANCES JOURNAL
PAGE 11

DATE	ACCOUNT CREDITED	CREDIT MEMO. NO.	POST. REF.	ACCOUNTS RECEIVABLE CREDIT	SALES TAX PAYABLE DEBIT	SALES RETURNS AND ALLOWANCES DEBIT — MEN'S CLOTHING	SALES RETURNS AND ALLOWANCES DEBIT — WOMEN'S CLOTHING

Chapter 2 Recording Departmental Sales and Cash Receipts

2-3 MASTERY PROBLEM (concluded)

[1, 3]

CASH RECEIPTS JOURNAL PAGE 11

DATE	ACCOUNT TITLE	DOC. NO.	POST. REF.	GENERAL DEBIT (1)	GENERAL CREDIT (2)	ACCOUNTS RECEIVABLE CREDIT (3)	SALES TAX PAYABLE DEBIT (4)	SALES TAX PAYABLE CREDIT (5)	SALES CREDIT MEN'S CLOTHING (6)	SALES CREDIT WOMEN'S CLOTHING (7)	SALES DISCOUNT DEBIT MEN'S CLOTHING (8)	SALES DISCOUNT DEBIT WOMEN'S CLOTHING (9)	CASH DEBIT (10)

46 • Working Papers

2-4 CHALLENGE PROBLEM, p. 59

Journalizing departmental sales, sales returns and allowances, and cash receipts   [1, 2]

SALES JOURNAL   PAGE 6

	DATE	ACCOUNT DEBITED	SALE NO.	POST. REF.	ACCOUNTS RECEIVABLE DEBIT	SALES CREDIT	
						MEN'S CLOTHING	WOMEN'S CLOTHING
1							
2							
3							
4							
5							
6							
7							
8							
9							
10							
11							

[1, 2]

SALES RETURNS AND ALLOWANCES JOURNAL   PAGE 6

	DATE	ACCOUNT CREDITED	CREDIT MEMO. NO.	POST. REF.	ACCOUNTS RECEIVABLE CREDIT	SALES RETURNS AND ALLOWANCES DEBIT	
						MEN'S CLOTHING	WOMEN'S CLOTHING
1							
2							
3							
4							
5							
6							
7							
8							
9							
10							
11							
12							
13							
14							
15							

2-4 CHALLENGE PROBLEM (concluded)

[1, 2]

CASH RECEIPTS JOURNAL PAGE 11

DATE	ACCOUNT TITLE	DOC. NO.	POST. REF.	GENERAL DEBIT	GENERAL CREDIT	ACCOUNTS RECEIVABLE CREDIT	SALES CREDIT MEN'S CLOTHING	SALES CREDIT WOMEN'S CLOTHING	SALES DISCOUNT DEBIT MEN'S CLOTHING	SALES DISCOUNT DEBIT WOMEN'S CLOTHING	CASH DEBIT

Name _____ Date _____ Class _____

3-1 WORK TOGETHER, p. 69

Preparing a benefits record; calculating employee earnings; preparing a commissions record

[4]

BENEFITS RECORD

EMPLOYEE NO. _____ EMPLOYEE NAME _____ DEPARTMENT _____

DATE OF INITIAL EMPLOYMENT _____ YEAR _____

	1	2	3	4	5	6	7	8	9	10	11	12
	VACATION TIME				SICK LEAVE TIME				PERSONAL LEAVE TIME			
PAY PERIOD ENDED	BEGIN. HOURS AVAIL.	HOURS EARNED	HOURS USED	ACC. HOURS AVAIL.	BEGIN. HOURS AVAIL.	HOURS EARNED	HOURS USED	ACC. HOURS AVAIL.	BEGIN. HOURS AVAIL.	HOURS EARNED	HOURS USED	ACC. HOURS AVAIL.
1												
2												
3												
4												
5												
6												
7												
8												
9												
10												
11												
12												
13												
14												
15												

[5]

EMPLOYEE EARNINGS

Employee Number	Hours Worked		Regular Rate	Earnings		Total Earnings
	Regular	Overtime		Regular	Overtime	

3-1 WORK TOGETHER (concluded)

[6]

COMMISSIONS RECORD

EMPLOYEE NO. _____   EMPLOYEE NAME _____

COMMISSION RATE _____   MONTH _____   YEAR _____

DEPT. _____   REGULAR BIWEEKLY SALARY _____

Sales

    Sales on Account . . . . $ _____

    Cash and Credit Card Sales . . . . _____

    Total Sales . . . . $ _____

    Less: Sales Discounts . . . . $ _____

        Sales Returns
        and Allowances . . . . _____   _____

    Net Sales . . . . $ _____

    Commission on Net Sales . . . . $ _____

Extra form

COMMISSIONS RECORD

EMPLOYEE NO. _____   EMPLOYEE NAME _____

COMMISSION RATE _____   MONTH _____   YEAR _____

DEPT. _____   REGULAR BIWEEKLY SALARY _____

Sales

    Sales on Account . . . . $ _____

    Cash and Credit Card Sales . . . . _____

    Total Sales . . . . $ _____

    Less: Sales Discounts . . . . $ _____

        Sales Returns
        and Allowances . . . . _____   _____

    Net Sales . . . . $ _____

    Commission on Net Sales . . . . $ _____

Name _____ Date _____ Class _____

3-1 ON YOUR OWN, p. 70

Preparing a benefits record; calculating employee earnings; [7]
preparing a commissions record

BENEFITS RECORD

EMPLOYEE NO. _____ EMPLOYEE NAME _____ DEPARTMENT _____

DATE OF INITIAL EMPLOYMENT _____ YEAR _____

	1	2	3	4	5	6	7	8	9	10	11	12
PAY PERIOD ENDED	VACATION TIME				SICK LEAVE TIME				PERSONAL LEAVE TIME			
	BEGIN. HOURS AVAIL.	HOURS EARNED	HOURS USED	ACC. HOURS AVAIL.	BEGIN. HOURS AVAIL.	HOURS EARNED	HOURS USED	ACC. HOURS AVAIL.	BEGIN. HOURS AVAIL.	HOURS EARNED	HOURS USED	ACC. HOURS AVAIL.
1												
2												
3												
4												
5												
6												
7												
8												
9												
10												
11												
12												
13												
14												
15												

[8]

EMPLOYEE EARNINGS

Employee Number	Hours Worked		Regular Rate	Earnings		Total Earnings
	Regular	Overtime		Regular	Overtime	

Name _____ Date _____ Class _____

3-1 ON YOUR OWN (continued)

[9]

```
┌─────────────────────────────────────────────────────────────────────┐
│                         COMMISSIONS RECORD                          │
│                                                                     │
│   EMPLOYEE NO. _____    EMPLOYEE NAME _____   │
│                                                                     │
│   COMMISSION RATE _____    MONTH _____   YEAR _____  │
│                                                                     │
│   DEPT. _____    REGULAR BIWEEKLY SALARY _____  │
│ ═══════════════════════════════════════════════════════════════════ │
│                                                                     │
│   Sales                                                             │
│       Sales on Account...........................  $ _____       │
│       Cash and Credit Card Sales..................   _____       │
│       Total Sales................................  $ _____       │
│       Less: Sales Discounts..............  $_____                 │
│             Sales Returns                                           │
│             and Allowances...............   _____    _____     │
│       Net Sales..................................... $ _____     │
│       Commission on Net Sales....................... $ _____     │
└─────────────────────────────────────────────────────────────────────┘
```

Extra form

```
┌─────────────────────────────────────────────────────────────────────┐
│                         COMMISSIONS RECORD                          │
│                                                                     │
│   EMPLOYEE NO. _____    EMPLOYEE NAME _____   │
│                                                                     │
│   COMMISSION RATE _____    MONTH _____   YEAR _____  │
│                                                                     │
│   DEPT. _____    REGULAR BIWEEKLY SALARY _____  │
│ ═══════════════════════════════════════════════════════════════════ │
│                                                                     │
│   Sales                                                             │
│       Sales on Account...........................  $ _____       │
│       Cash and Credit Card Sales..................   _____       │
│       Total Sales................................  $ _____       │
│       Less: Sales Discounts..............  $_____                 │
│             Sales Returns                                           │
│             and Allowances...............   _____    _____     │
│       Net Sales..................................... $ _____     │
│       Commission on Net Sales....................... $ _____     │
└─────────────────────────────────────────────────────────────────────┘
```

Name ______________________ Date ______________ Class ______________

3-2 WORK TOGETHER

(Note: The payroll register for this problem begins on page 54.)

Extra forms

PAYROLL REGISTER

DATE OF PAYMENT

	10	11	12	13	14	15	16	17	18	19	20	
	DEPARTMENT		ADMIN. SALARIES	DEDUCTIONS						PAID		
	HARDWARE	PAINT		FEDERAL INCOME TAX	STATE INCOME TAX	SOC. SEC. TAX	MEDICARE TAX	OTHER	TOTAL	NET PAY	CHECK NO.	
1												1
2												2
3												3
4												4
5												5
6												6
7												7
8												8
9												9
10												10
11												11
12												12
13												13
14												14
15												15

PAYROLL REGISTER

DATE OF PAYMENT

	10	11	12	13	14	15	16	17	18	19	20	
	DEPARTMENT		ADMIN. SALARIES	DEDUCTIONS						PAID		
	HARDWARE	PAINT		FEDERAL INCOME TAX	STATE INCOME TAX	SOC. SEC. TAX	MEDICARE TAX	OTHER	TOTAL	NET PAY	CHECK NO.	
1												1
2												2
3												3
4												4
5												5
6												6
7												7
8												8
9												9
10												10
11												11
12												12
13												13
14												14
15												15

3-2 WORK TOGETHER, p. 77

Completing payroll records [5, 6]

PAYROLL REGISTER
PAY PERIOD ENDED 7/3/20--

EMPL. NO.	EMPLOYEE NAME	MARITAL STATUS	NO. OF ALLOWANCES	TOTAL HOURS	EARNINGS REGULAR	OVERTIME	COMMISSION	TOTAL
1								
2								
3								
4								
5								
6								
7								
8								
9								
10								
11								
12								
13								
14								
15					1,418.00	776.40	582.00	1,553.840

[7]

EARNINGS RECORD FOR QUARTER ENDED Sept. 30, 20--

EMPLOYEE NO. 4 NAME Fulton, Susan SOCIAL SECURITY NO. 555-72-5782
MARITAL STATUS S WITHHOLDING ALLOWANCES 1 HOURLY RATE $10.00 SALARY ____
DEPARTMENT Hardware POSITION Salesclerk

PAY PERIOD NO.	ENDED	TOTAL EARNINGS	DEDUCTIONS FEDERAL INCOME TAX	STATE INCOME TAX	SOC. SEC. TAX	MEDICARE TAX	OTHER	TOTAL	NET PAY	ACCUMULATED EARNINGS
1										
2										
3										
4										
5										
6										
7										
8										
9										
10										

3-2 WORK TOGETHER (concluded)

[5, 6]

PAYROLL REGISTER

DATE OF PAYMENT 7/10/20--

	DEPARTMENT		ADMIN. SALARIES	DEDUCTIONS						PAID	
	HARDWARE	PAINT		FEDERAL INCOME TAX	STATE INCOME TAX	SOC. SEC. TAX	MEDICARE TAX	OTHER	TOTAL	NET PAY	CHECK NO.
1											
2											
3											
4											
5											
6											
7											
8											
9											
10											
11											
12											
13											
14											
15	7605.80	5070.60	2862.00	1305.00	776.92	1010.00	233.08	H 588.00 L 102.40	4015.40	11523.00	

Extra form

EARNINGS RECORD FOR QUARTER ENDED _____

EMPLOYEE NO. _____ NAME _____ SOCIAL SECURITY NO. _____

MARITAL STATUS _____ WITHHOLDING ALLOWANCES _____ HOURLY RATE _____ SALARY _____

DEPARTMENT _____ POSITION _____

PAY PERIOD		TOTAL EARNINGS	DEDUCTIONS						NET PAY	ACCUMULATED EARNINGS
NO.	ENDED		FEDERAL INCOME TAX	STATE INCOME TAX	SOC. SEC. TAX	MEDICARE TAX	OTHER	TOTAL		
1										
2										
3										
4										
5										
6										
7										
8										
9										
10										

Name ____________________ Date __________ Class __________

3-2 WORK TOGETHER

Extra forms

PAY PERIOD ENDED

PAYROLL REGISTER

	1	2	3	4	5	6	7	8	9	
						EARNINGS				
	EMPL. NO.	EMPLOYEE NAME	MARITAL STATUS	NO. OF ALLOWANCES	TOTAL HOURS	REGULAR	OVERTIME	COMMISSION	TOTAL	
1										1
2										2
3										3
4										4
5										5
6										6
7										7
8										8
9										9
10										10
11										11
12										12
13										13
14										14
15										15

PAY PERIOD ENDED

PAYROLL REGISTER

	1	2	3	4	5	6	7	8	9	
						EARNINGS				
	EMPL. NO.	EMPLOYEE NAME	MARITAL STATUS	NO. OF ALLOWANCES	TOTAL HOURS	REGULAR	OVERTIME	COMMISSION	TOTAL	
1										1
2										2
3										3
4										4
5										5
6										6
7										7
8										8
9										9
10										10
11										11
12										12
13										13
14										14
15										15

3-2 ON YOUR OWN

(Note: The payroll register for this problem begins on page 58.)

Extra forms

DATE OF PAYMENT	PAYROLL REGISTER									
	DEPARTMENT		ADMIN. SALARIES	DEDUCTIONS					PAID	
	HARDWARE	PAINT		FEDERAL INCOME TAX	STATE INCOME TAX	SOC. SEC. TAX	MEDICARE TAX	OTHER	TOTAL	NET PAY	CHECK NO.

3-2 ON YOUR OWN, page 78

Completing payroll records [8, 9]

PAYROLL REGISTER

PAY PERIOD ENDED 10/2/20--

EMPL. NO.	EMPLOYEE NAME	MARITAL STATUS	NO. OF ALLOWANCES	TOTAL HOURS	REGULAR	OVERTIME	COMMISSION	TOTAL	
1									1
2									2
3									3
4									4
5									5
6									6
7									7
8									8
9									9
10									10
11									11
12									12
13									13
14									14
15					1490 00	815 00	611 00	1632 6 00	15

[10]

EARNINGS RECORD FOR QUARTER ENDED Dec. 31, 20--

EMPLOYEE NO. 12   NAME Parker, Keith   SOCIAL SECURITY NO. 555-75-1782
MARITAL STATUS S   WITHHOLDING ALLOWANCES 1   HOURLY RATE $9.50   SALARY _____
DEPARTMENT Paint   POSITION Salesclerk

PAY PERIOD		TOTAL EARNINGS	FEDERAL INCOME TAX	STATE INCOME TAX	SOC. SEC. TAX	MEDICARE TAX	OTHER	TOTAL	NET PAY	ACCUMULATED EARNINGS
NO.	ENDED									
1										
2										
3										
4										
5										
6										
7										
8										
9										
10										

3-2 ON YOUR OWN (concluded)

[8, 9]

PAYROLL REGISTER

DATE OF PAYMENT 10/9/20--

| | DEPARTMENT || ADMIN. SALARIES | DEDUCTIONS |||||| PAID ||
	HARDWARE	PAINT		FEDERAL INCOME TAX	STATE INCOME TAX	SOC. SEC. TAX	MEDICARE TAX	OTHER	TOTAL	NET PAY	CHECK NO.
1											
2											
3											
4											
5											
6											
7											
8											
9											
10											
11											
12											
13											
14											
15	7266 00	5945 00	3115 00	1388 00	816 30	1061 19	244 89	H 588 00 L 102 40	4200 78	12125 22	

Extra form

EARNINGS RECORD FOR QUARTER ENDED _____

EMPLOYEE NO. _____ NAME _____ SOCIAL SECURITY NO. _____

MARITAL STATUS _____ WITHHOLDING ALLOWANCES _____ HOURLY RATE _____ SALARY _____

DEPARTMENT _____ POSITION _____

| PAY PERIOD || TOTAL EARNINGS | DEDUCTIONS |||||| NET PAY | ACCUMULATED EARNINGS |
NO.	ENDED		FEDERAL INCOME TAX	STATE INCOME TAX	SOC. SEC. TAX	MEDICARE TAX	OTHER	TOTAL		
1										
2										
3										
4										
5										
6										
7										
8										
9										
10										

Name ____________________ Date __________ Class __________

3-2 ON YOUR OWN

Extra forms

PAY PERIOD ENDED

PAYROLL REGISTER

	1	2	3	4	5	6	7	8	9	
						EARNINGS				
	EMPL. NO.	EMPLOYEE NAME	MARI-TAL STATUS	NO. OF ALLOW-ANCES	TOTAL HOURS	REGULAR	OVERTIME	COMMISSION	TOTAL	
1										1
2										2
3										3
4										4
5										5
6										6
7										7
8										8
9										9
10										10
11										11
12										12
13										13
14										14
15										15

PAY PERIOD ENDED

PAYROLL REGISTER

	1	2	3	4	5	6	7	8	9	
						EARNINGS				
	EMPL. NO.	EMPLOYEE NAME	MARI-TAL STATUS	NO. OF ALLOW-ANCES	TOTAL HOURS	REGULAR	OVERTIME	COMMISSION	TOTAL	
1										1
2										2
3										3
4										4
5										5
6										6
7										7
8										8
9										9
10										10
11										11
12										12
13										13
14										14
15										15

3-3 WORK TOGETHER, p. 84

Journalizing and paying payroll and payroll taxes [3]

(Blank Cash Payments Journal form)

3-3 WORK TOGETHER (concluded)

[3]

GENERAL JOURNAL

PAGE

	DATE	ACCOUNT TITLE	DOC. NO.	POST. REF.	DEBIT	CREDIT	
1							1
2							2
3							3
4							4
5							5
6							6
7							7
8							8
9							9
10							10
11							11
12							12
13							13
14							14
15							15
16							16
17							17
18							18
19							19
20							20
21							21
22							22
23							23
24							24
25							25
26							26
27							27
28							28
29							29
30							30
31							31

62 • Working Papers

COPYRIGHT © SOUTH-WESTERN EDUCATIONAL PUBLISHING

3-3 ON YOUR OWN, p. 84

Journalizing and paying payroll and payroll taxes [4]

CASH PAYMENTS JOURNAL (blank form)

3-3 ON YOUR OWN (concluded)

[4]

GENERAL JOURNAL

PAGE

	DATE	ACCOUNT TITLE	DOC. NO.	POST. REF.	DEBIT	CREDIT	
1							1
2							2
3							3
4							4
5							5
6							6
7							7
8							8
9							9
10							10
11							11
12							12
13							13
14							14
15							15
16							16
17							17
18							18
19							19
20							20
21							21
22							22
23							23
24							24
25							25
26							26
27							27
28							28
29							29
30							30
31							31

3-1 APPLICATION PROBLEM, p. 86

Preparing a benefits record

BENEFITS RECORD

EMPLOYEE NO. _____ EMPLOYEE NAME _____ DEPARTMENT _____

DATE OF INITIAL EMPLOYMENT _____ YEAR _____

PAY PERIOD ENDED	VACATION TIME				SICK LEAVE TIME				PERSONAL LEAVE TIME			
	BEGIN. HOURS AVAIL.	HOURS EARNED	HOURS USED	ACC. HOURS AVAIL.	BEGIN. HOURS AVAIL.	HOURS EARNED	HOURS USED	ACC. HOURS AVAIL.	BEGIN. HOURS AVAIL.	HOURS EARNED	HOURS USED	ACC. HOURS AVAIL.
1												
2												
3												
4												
5												
6												
7												
8												
9												
10												
11												
12												
13												
14												
15												

Extra form

BENEFITS RECORD

EMPLOYEE NO. _____ EMPLOYEE NAME _____ DEPARTMENT _____

DATE OF INITIAL EMPLOYMENT _____ YEAR _____

PAY PERIOD ENDED	VACATION TIME				SICK LEAVE TIME				PERSONAL LEAVE TIME			
	BEGIN. HOURS AVAIL.	HOURS EARNED	HOURS USED	ACC. HOURS AVAIL.	BEGIN. HOURS AVAIL.	HOURS EARNED	HOURS USED	ACC. HOURS AVAIL.	BEGIN. HOURS AVAIL.	HOURS EARNED	HOURS USED	ACC. HOURS AVAIL.
1												
2												
3												
4												
5												
6												
7												
8												
9												
10												
11												
12												
13												
14												
15												
16												

Chapter 3 Calculating and Recording Departmental Payroll Data

Name _____ Date _____ Class _____

3-1 APPLICATION PROBLEM

Extra forms

BENEFITS RECORD

EMPLOYEE NO. _____ EMPLOYEE NAME _____ DEPARTMENT _____

DATE OF INITIAL EMPLOYMENT _____ YEAR _____

PAY PERIOD ENDED	VACATION TIME				SICK LEAVE TIME				PERSONAL LEAVE TIME			
	BEGIN. HOURS AVAIL.	HOURS EARNED	HOURS USED	ACC. HOURS AVAIL.	BEGIN. HOURS AVAIL.	HOURS EARNED	HOURS USED	ACC. HOURS AVAIL.	BEGIN. HOURS AVAIL.	HOURS EARNED	HOURS USED	ACC. HOURS AVAIL.
1												
2												
3												
4												
5												
6												
7												
8												
9												
10												
11												
12												
13												
14												
15												
16												

BENEFITS RECORD

EMPLOYEE NO. _____ EMPLOYEE NAME _____ DEPARTMENT _____

DATE OF INITIAL EMPLOYMENT _____ YEAR _____

PAY PERIOD ENDED	VACATION TIME				SICK LEAVE TIME				PERSONAL LEAVE TIME			
	BEGIN. HOURS AVAIL.	HOURS EARNED	HOURS USED	ACC. HOURS AVAIL.	BEGIN. HOURS AVAIL.	HOURS EARNED	HOURS USED	ACC. HOURS AVAIL.	BEGIN. HOURS AVAIL.	HOURS EARNED	HOURS USED	ACC. HOURS AVAIL.
1												
2												
3												
4												
5												
6												
7												
8												
9												
10												
11												
12												
13												
14												
15												
16												

Name _____ Date _____ Class _____

3-2 APPLICATION PROBLEM, p. 86

Recording employee benefits and calculating earnings on time cards

BENEFITS AUTHORIZATION

EMPLOYEE NO. __3__   EMPLOYEE __Janet T. Aguilar__

PAY PERIOD ENDED __3/12/--__   DEPARTMENT __Carpet__

	HOURS AVAIL.	M	T	W	T	F	S	M	T	W	T	F	S	HOURS USED
VACATION	64			4					4					8
SICK LEAVE	46				4									4
PERSONAL LEAVE	12											2		2

_____   Eileen S. Johnson   __3/12/--__
MANAGER (only if needed)   DEPARTMENT SUPERVISOR   DATE

BENEFITS AUTHORIZATION

EMPLOYEE NO. __8__   EMPLOYEE __Bernard C. Parker__

PAY PERIOD ENDED __3/12/--__   DEPARTMENT __Administrative__

	HOURS AVAIL.	M	T	W	T	F	S	M	T	W	T	F	S	HOURS USED
VACATION	52	8												8
SICK LEAVE	30								8	4				12
PERSONAL LEAVE	17			2								1		3

Belinda F. Pullen   _____   __3/12/--__
MANAGER (only if needed)   DEPARTMENT SUPERVISOR   DATE

BENEFITS AUTHORIZATION

EMPLOYEE NO. __13__   EMPLOYEE __Natalie R. Sabo__

PAY PERIOD ENDED __3/12/--__   DEPARTMENT __Drapery__

	HOURS AVAIL.	M	T	W	T	F	S	M	T	W	T	F	S	HOURS USED
VACATION	68				8	8	8							24
SICK LEAVE	47											4		4
PERSONAL LEAVE	20										4			4

_____   Paul T. Burke   __3/12/--__
MANAGER (only if needed)   DEPARTMENT SUPERVISOR   DATE

Name _____ Date _____ Class _____

3-2 APPLICATION PROBLEM (continued)

[1]

BENEFITS RECORD

EMPLOYEE NO. **3**   EMPLOYEE NAME **Janet T. Aquilar**   DEPARTMENT **Carpet**

DATE OF INITIAL EMPLOYMENT **February 8, 19--**   YEAR **20--**

	1	2	3	4	5	6	7	8	9	10	11	12
PAY PERIOD ENDED	VACATION TIME				SICK LEAVE TIME				PERSONAL LEAVE TIME			
	BEGIN. HOURS AVAIL.	HOURS EARNED	HOURS USED	ACC. HOURS AVAIL.	BEGIN. HOURS AVAIL.	HOURS EARNED	HOURS USED	ACC. HOURS AVAIL.	BEGIN. HOURS AVAIL.	HOURS EARNED	HOURS USED	ACC. HOURS AVAIL.
6												
7												
8												
9												
10												
11												

BENEFITS RECORD

EMPLOYEE NO. **8**   EMPLOYEE NAME **Bernard C. Parker**   DEPARTMENT **Administrative**

DATE OF INITIAL EMPLOYMENT **July 16, 19--**   YEAR **20--**

	1	2	3	4	5	6	7	8	9	10	11	12
PAY PERIOD ENDED	VACATION TIME				SICK LEAVE TIME				PERSONAL LEAVE TIME			
	BEGIN. HOURS AVAIL.	HOURS EARNED	HOURS USED	ACC. HOURS AVAIL.	BEGIN. HOURS AVAIL.	HOURS EARNED	HOURS USED	ACC. HOURS AVAIL.	BEGIN. HOURS AVAIL.	HOURS EARNED	HOURS USED	ACC. HOURS AVAIL.
6												
7												
8												
9												
10												
11												

BENEFITS RECORD

EMPLOYEE NO. **13**   EMPLOYEE NAME **Natalie R. Sabo**   DEPARTMENT **Drapery**

DATE OF INITIAL EMPLOYMENT **March 11, 19--**   YEAR **20--**

	1	2	3	4	5	6	7	8	9	10	11	12
PAY PERIOD ENDED	VACATION TIME				SICK LEAVE TIME				PERSONAL LEAVE TIME			
	BEGIN. HOURS AVAIL.	HOURS EARNED	HOURS USED	ACC. HOURS AVAIL.	BEGIN. HOURS AVAIL.	HOURS EARNED	HOURS USED	ACC. HOURS AVAIL.	BEGIN. HOURS AVAIL.	HOURS EARNED	HOURS USED	ACC. HOURS AVAIL.
6												
7												
8												
9												
10												
11												

3-2 APPLICATION PROBLEM (continued)

The time cards prepared in this problem are needed to complete Application Problem 3-4.   [2–4]

NAME **Janet T. Aguilar**
DEPARTMENT **Carpet**
EMPLOYEE NO. **3**
PAY PERIOD ENDED **3/12/20--**

MORNING		AFTERNOON		OVERTIME		HOURS	
IN	OUT	IN	OUT	IN	OUT	REG	OT
9:01	11:59	1:00	6:03				
9:00	12:01	1:00	6:00	7:00	9:00		
8:58	12:00	1:01	2:03				
9:02	12:01	1:00	6:00	7:30	9:00		
		2:00	6:01				
9:01	12:00	1:00	6:01				
9:00	12:01	1:01	2:01				
9:00	12:00	1:00	6:01	7:30	8:30		
9:01	12:00	1:01	6:00				
9:00	12:00	1:02	4:00				

	HOURS	RATE	AMOUNT
REGULAR		7.00	
OVERTIME			
TOTAL HOURS		TOTAL EARNINGS	

NAME **Bernard C. Parker**
DEPARTMENT **Administrative**
EMPLOYEE NO. **8**
PAY PERIOD ENDED **3/12/20--**

MORNING		AFTERNOON		OVERTIME		HOURS	
IN	OUT	IN	OUT	IN	OUT	REG	OT
9:00	12:01	1:00	6:00	7:00	8:30		
8:59	12:00	12:58	4:00				
9:01	12:00	1:02	6:03	7:30	9:00		
9:00	12:02	1:01	6:00				
		2:00	6:02				
8:58	12:01	1:01	6:00				
9:01	12:00	1:00	6:00	7:00	8:00		
9:00	12:02	1:00	5:00				

	HOURS	RATE	AMOUNT
REGULAR		6.50	
OVERTIME			
TOTAL HOURS		TOTAL EARNINGS	

3-2 APPLICATION PROBLEM (concluded)

The time cards prepared in this problem are needed to complete Application Problem 3-4.

Extra form

NAME	Natalie R. Sabo
DEPARTMENT	Drapery
EMPLOYEE NO.	13
PAY PERIOD ENDED	3/12/20--

MORNING		AFTERNOON		OVERTIME		HOURS	
IN	OUT	IN	OUT	IN	OUT	REG	OT
T 9:00	T 12:59	T 2:00	T 6:02	T 7:00	T 8:00		
W 9:01	W 1:00	W 2:00	W 6:01				
T 9:00	T 1:03	T 2:00	T 6:00	T 7:00	T 9:30		
W 8:58	W 1:00	W 2:01	W 6:01				
T 9:00	T 1:03						
F 9:00	F 1:00	F 2:02	F 6:03	F 7:00	F 8:00		
S 9:03	S 1:00						

	HOURS	RATE	AMOUNT
REGULAR		6.50	
OVERTIME			
TOTAL HOURS		TOTAL EARNINGS	

NAME	
DEPARTMENT	
EMPLOYEE NO.	
PAY PERIOD ENDED	

MORNING		AFTERNOON		OVERTIME		HOURS	
IN	OUT	IN	OUT	IN	OUT	REG	OT
S	S	S	S				
M	M	M	M				
T	T	T	T				
W	W	W	W				
T	T	T	T				
F	F	F	F				
S	S	S	S				
S	S	S	S				
M	M	M	M				
T	T	T	T				
W	W	W	W				
T	T	T	T				
F	F	F	F				
S	S	S	S				

	HOURS	RATE	AMOUNT
REGULAR			
OVERTIME			
TOTAL HOURS		TOTAL EARNINGS	

Name _____ Date _____ Class _____

3-3 APPLICATION PROBLEM, p. 86

Preparing departmental commissions records

The commissions records prepared in this problem are needed to complete Application Problem 3-4.

COMMISSIONS RECORD

EMPLOYEE NO. _____   EMPLOYEE NAME _____

COMMISSION RATE _____   MONTH _____   YEAR _____

DEPT. _____   REGULAR BIWEEKLY SALARY _____

Sales

    Sales on Account . . . . $ _____

    Cash and Credit Card Sales . . . . _____

    Total Sales . . . . $ _____

    Less: Sales Discounts . . . . $ _____

        Sales Returns
        and Allowances . . . . _____   _____

    Net Sales . . . . $ _____

    Commission on Net Sales . . . . $ _____

COMMISSIONS RECORD

EMPLOYEE NO. _____   EMPLOYEE NAME _____

COMMISSION RATE _____   MONTH _____   YEAR _____

DEPT. _____   REGULAR BIWEEKLY SALARY _____

Sales

    Sales on Account . . . . $ _____

    Cash and Credit Card Sales . . . . _____

    Total Sales . . . . $ _____

    Less: Sales Discounts . . . . $ _____

        Sales Returns
        and Allowances . . . . _____   _____

    Net Sales . . . . $ _____

    Commission on Net Sales . . . . $ _____

Name _____ Date _____ Class _____

3-3 APPLICATION PROBLEM

Extra forms

COMMISSIONS RECORD

EMPLOYEE NO. _____ EMPLOYEE NAME _____

COMMISSION RATE _____ MONTH _____ YEAR _____

DEPT. _____ REGULAR BIWEEKLY SALARY _____

Sales

    Sales on Account . . . . $ _____

    Cash and Credit Card Sales . . . . _____

    Total Sales . . . . $ _____

    Less: Sales Discounts . . . . $ _____

        Sales Returns
        and Allowances . . . . _____   _____

    Net Sales . . . . $ _____

    Commission on Net Sales . . . . $ _____

COMMISSIONS RECORD

EMPLOYEE NO. _____ EMPLOYEE NAME _____

COMMISSION RATE _____ MONTH _____ YEAR _____

DEPT. _____ REGULAR BIWEEKLY SALARY _____

Sales

    Sales on Account . . . . $ _____

    Cash and Credit Card Sales . . . . _____

    Total Sales . . . . $ _____

    Less: Sales Discounts . . . . $ _____

        Sales Returns
        and Allowances . . . . _____   _____

    Net Sales . . . . $ _____

    Commission on Net Sales . . . . $ _____

Name _____ Date _____ Class _____

3-5 APPLICATION PROBLEM, p. 87

Completing an employee earnings record

The payroll register prepared in Application Problem 3-4 is needed to complete this problem.

The working papers for Application Problem 3-4 are located on pages 74 and 75.

EARNINGS RECORD FOR QUARTER ENDED March 31, 20--

EMPLOYEE NO. 3 NAME Janet T. Aquilar SOCIAL SECURITY NO. 013-62-1432
MARITAL STATUS M WITHHOLDING ALLOWANCES 3 HOURLY RATE $7.00 SALARY _____
DEPARTMENT Carpet POSITION Sales clerk

1	2	3	4	5	6	7	8	9	10	11
PAY PERIOD		TOTAL EARNINGS	DEDUCTIONS						NET PAY	ACCUMULATED EARNINGS
NO.	ENDED		FEDERAL INCOME TAX	STATE INCOME TAX	SOC. SEC. TAX	MEDICARE TAX	OTHER	TOTAL		
5	2/27	560.00	2.00	28.00	36.40	8.40	DH 13.20 / 9.40	97.40	462.60	3050.25
6										
QUARTERLY TOTALS										

EARNINGS RECORD FOR QUARTER ENDED March 31, 20--

EMPLOYEE NO. 8 NAME Bernard C. Parker SOCIAL SECURITY NO. 181-48-0482
MARITAL STATUS M WITHHOLDING ALLOWANCES 2 HOURLY RATE $6.50 SALARY _____
DEPARTMENT Administrative POSITION Clerk

1	2	3	4	5	6	7	8	9	10	11
PAY PERIOD		TOTAL EARNINGS	DEDUCTIONS						NET PAY	ACCUMULATED EARNINGS
NO.	ENDED		FEDERAL INCOME TAX	STATE INCOME TAX	SOC. SEC. TAX	MEDICARE TAX	OTHER	TOTAL		
5	2/27	520.00	12.00	26.00	33.80	7.80	DH 13.20 / 9.40	102.20	417.80	2784.10
6										
QUARTERLY TOTALS										

3-4 APPLICATION PROBLEM, p. 87

Completing a payroll register

The time cards prepared in Application Problem 3-2 and the commissions records prepared in Application Problem 3-3 are needed to complete this problem. The payroll register prepared in Application Problem 3-4 is needed to complete Application Problems 3-5 and 3-6.

PAY PERIOD ENDED March 12, 20--   PAYROLL REGISTER

	EMPL. NO.	EMPLOYEE NAME	MARITAL STATUS	NO. OF ALLOWANCES	TOTAL HOURS	EARNINGS REGULAR	EARNINGS OVERTIME	EARNINGS COMMISSION	EARNINGS TOTAL	
1	3	Aguilar, Janet T.	M	3						1
2	9	Gowens, Heidi	S	1						2
3	14	Mantle, Dale	M	2						3
4	8	Parker, Bernard C.	M	2						4
5	13	Sabo, Natalie R.	S	2						5
6										6
7										7
8										8
9										9

3-5 APPLICATION PROBLEM (continued)

EARNINGS RECORD FOR QUARTER ENDED March 31, 20--

EMPLOYEE NO. 9   NAME Heidi Gowens   SOCIAL SECURITY NO. 311-32-1620
MARITAL STATUS S   WITHHOLDING ALLOWANCES 1   HOURLY RATE _____   SALARY $540.00
DEPARTMENT Carpet   POSITION Supervisor

PAY PERIOD NO.	ENDED	TOTAL EARNINGS	DEDUCTIONS FEDERAL INCOME TAX	STATE INCOME TAX	SOC. SEC. TAX	MEDICARE TAX	OTHER		TOTAL	NET PAY	ACCUMULATED EARNINGS
5	2/27	540 00	52 00	27 00	35 10	8 10	D H	9 40 13 20	144 80	395 20	3165 20
6											
QUARTERLY TOTALS											

Name _____ Date _____ Class _____

3-4 APPLICATION PROBLEM (concluded)

PAYROLL REGISTER

DATE OF PAYMENT: March 19, 20--

| | DEPARTMENT | | ADMIN. SALARIES | DEDUCTIONS | | | | | | PAID | |
	CARPET	DRAPERY		FEDERAL INCOME TAX	STATE INCOME TAX	SOC. SEC. TAX	MEDICARE TAX	OTHER	TOTAL	NET PAY	CHECK NO.
1											
2											
3											
4											
5											
6											
7											
8											
9											

(Columns numbered 10–20)

3-5 APPLICATION PROBLEM (continued)

EARNINGS RECORD FOR QUARTER ENDED March 31, 20--

EMPLOYEE NO. 13 NAME Natalie R. Sabo SOCIAL SECURITY NO. 214-36-1832

MARITAL STATUS S WITHHOLDING ALLOWANCES 2 HOURLY RATE $6.50 SALARY _____

DEPARTMENT Drapery POSITION Salesclerk

| PAY PERIOD | | TOTAL EARNINGS | DEDUCTIONS | | | | | TOTAL | NET PAY | ACCUMULATED EARNINGS |
NO.	ENDED		FEDERAL INCOME TAX	STATE INCOME TAX	SOC. SEC. TAX	MEDICARE TAX	OTHER			
5	2/27	520.00	34.00	26.00	33.80	7.80	DH 13 9.40 20	124.20	395.80	2,676.90
6										
QUARTERLY TOTALS										

Name _____ Date _____ Class _____

3-5 APPLICATION PROBLEM (concluded)

EARNINGS RECORD FOR QUARTER ENDED March 31, 20--

EMPLOYEE NO. 14 NAME Dale Mantle SOCIAL SECURITY NO. 192-40-2162
MARITAL STATUS M WITHHOLDING ALLOWANCES 2 HOURLY RATE ____ SALARY $520.00
DEPARTMENT Drapery POSITION Supervisor

PAY PERIOD		TOTAL EARNINGS	DEDUCTIONS						NET PAY	ACCUMULATED EARNINGS
NO.	ENDED		FEDERAL INCOME TAX	STATE INCOME TAX	SOC. SEC. TAX	MEDICARE TAX	OTHER	TOTAL		
5	2/27	520.00	12.00	26.00	33.80	7.80	DH 9.40 / 13.20	102.20	417.80	3094.30
6										
QUARTERLY TOTALS										

Extra forms

EARNINGS RECORD FOR QUARTER ENDED _____

EMPLOYEE NO. ____ NAME ____ SOCIAL SECURITY NO. ____
MARITAL STATUS ____ WITHHOLDING ALLOWANCES ____ HOURLY RATE ____ SALARY ____
DEPARTMENT ____ POSITION ____

PAY PERIOD		TOTAL EARNINGS	DEDUCTIONS						NET PAY	ACCUMULATED EARNINGS
NO.	ENDED		FEDERAL INCOME TAX	STATE INCOME TAX	SOC. SEC. TAX	MEDICARE TAX	OTHER	TOTAL		
5										
6										
QUARTERLY TOTALS										

EARNINGS RECORD FOR QUARTER ENDED _____

EMPLOYEE NO. ____ NAME ____ SOCIAL SECURITY NO. ____
MARITAL STATUS ____ WITHHOLDING ALLOWANCES ____ HOURLY RATE ____ SALARY ____
DEPARTMENT ____ POSITION ____

PAY PERIOD		TOTAL EARNINGS	DEDUCTIONS						NET PAY	ACCUMULATED EARNINGS
NO.	ENDED		FEDERAL INCOME TAX	STATE INCOME TAX	SOC. SEC. TAX	MEDICARE TAX	OTHER	TOTAL		
5										
6										
QUARTERLY TOTALS										

3-6 APPLICATION PROBLEM, p. 88

Journalizing payment of a departmental payroll

The payroll register prepared in Application Problem 3-4 is needed to complete this problem.

[1] CASH PAYMENTS JOURNAL — PAGE 6

[2] GENERAL JOURNAL — PAGE 6

3-6 APPLICATION PROBLEM

Extra forms

CASH PAYMENTS JOURNAL

DATE	ACCOUNT TITLE	CK. NO.	POST. REF.	GENERAL DEBIT	GENERAL CREDIT	ACCOUNTS PAYABLE DEBIT	PURCH. DISCOUNT CR. CARPET	PURCH. DISCOUNT CR. DRAPERY	CASH CREDIT

GENERAL JOURNAL

DATE	ACCOUNT TITLE	DOC. NO.	POST. REF.	DEBIT	CREDIT

3-7 APPLICATION PROBLEM, p. 88

Calculating and journalizing payment of payroll tax liabilities

[1] CASH PAYMENTS JOURNAL — PAGE 7

[2, 3] CASH PAYMENTS JOURNAL — PAGE 8

3-7 APPLICATION PROBLEM

Extra forms

Cash Payments Journal and General Journal — blank forms

Name _____ Date _____ Class _____

3-8 MASTERY PROBLEM, p. 88

Completing payroll records, journalizing payment of a payroll, and journalizing payroll taxes

BENEFITS AUTHORIZATION

EMPLOYEE NO. __1__   EMPLOYEE __Shanna L. Kim__

PAY PERIOD ENDED __2/13/--__   DEPARTMENT __Fabrics__

	HOURS AVAIL.	M	T	W	T	F	S	M	T	W	T	F	S	HOURS USED
VACATION	62					4								4
SICK LEAVE	42										1	5		6
PERSONAL LEAVE	20		4											4

_____   __Paula D. Brown__   __2/13/--__
MANAGER (only if needed)   DEPARTMENT SUPERVISOR   DATE

BENEFITS AUTHORIZATION

EMPLOYEE NO. __2__   EMPLOYEE __Paula D. Brown__

PAY PERIOD ENDED __2/13/--__   DEPARTMENT __Fabrics__

	HOURS AVAIL.	M	T	W	T	F	S	M	T	W	T	F	S	HOURS USED
VACATION	81										4			4
SICK LEAVE	72				8									8
PERSONAL LEAVE	22													0

__Maria C. Lucio__   _____   __2/13/--__
MANAGER (only if needed)   DEPARTMENT SUPERVISOR   DATE

BENEFITS AUTHORIZATION

EMPLOYEE NO. __3__   EMPLOYEE __Gary M. Evans__

PAY PERIOD ENDED __2/13/--__   DEPARTMENT __Supplies__

	HOURS AVAIL.	M	T	W	T	F	S	M	T	W	T	F	S	HOURS USED
VACATION	78	8												8
SICK LEAVE	52				5									5
PERSONAL LEAVE	20								3					3

_____   __Marcel P. Ostenbauer__   __2/13/--__
MANAGER (only if needed)   DEPARTMENT SUPERVISOR   DATE

3-8 MASTERY PROBLEM (continued)

BENEFITS AUTHORIZATION

EMPLOYEE NO. 4 EMPLOYEE Marcel P. Ostenbauer
PAY PERIOD ENDED 2/13/-- DEPARTMENT Supplies

	HOURS AVAIL.	M	T	W	T	F	S	M	T	W	T	F	S	HOURS USED
VACATION	80				8	8		8						24
SICK LEAVE	52											4		4
PERSONAL LEAVE	16										3			3

Maria C. Lucio
MANAGER (only if needed)   DEPARTMENT SUPERVISOR   2/13/-- DATE

BENEFITS AUTHORIZATION

EMPLOYEE NO. 5 EMPLOYEE Jean R. Quigley
PAY PERIOD ENDED 2/13/-- DEPARTMENT Fabrics

	HOURS AVAIL.	M	T	W	T	F	S	M	T	W	T	F	S	HOURS USED
VACATION	38											8	8	16
SICK LEAVE	70			4										4
PERSONAL LEAVE	18										2			2

                                   Paula D. Brown   2/13/--
MANAGER (only if needed)   DEPARTMENT SUPERVISOR   DATE

BENEFITS AUTHORIZATION

EMPLOYEE NO. 6 EMPLOYEE Robert J. Trumpley
PAY PERIOD ENDED 2/13/-- DEPARTMENT Administrative

	HOURS AVAIL.	M	T	W	T	F	S	M	T	W	T	F	S	HOURS USED
VACATION	50	8												8
SICK LEAVE	52											4		4
PERSONAL LEAVE	22					3								3

Maria C. Lucio
MANAGER (only if needed)   DEPARTMENT SUPERVISOR   2/13/-- DATE

Name _____ Date _____ Class _____

3-8 MASTERY PROBLEM (continued)

[1]

BENEFITS RECORD

EMPLOYEE NO. __1__   EMPLOYEE NAME __Shanna L. Kim__   DEPARTMENT __Fabrics__
DATE OF INITIAL EMPLOYMENT __April 16, 19--__   YEAR __20--__

PAY PERIOD ENDED	VACATION TIME				SICK LEAVE TIME				PERSONAL LEAVE TIME			
	BEGIN. HOURS AVAIL.	HOURS EARNED	HOURS USED	ACC. HOURS AVAIL.	BEGIN. HOURS AVAIL.	HOURS EARNED	HOURS USED	ACC. HOURS AVAIL.	BEGIN. HOURS AVAIL.	HOURS EARNED	HOURS USED	ACC. HOURS AVAIL.
4												
5												
6												
7												
8												
9												

BENEFITS RECORD

EMPLOYEE NO. __2__   EMPLOYEE NAME __Paula D. Brown__   DEPARTMENT __Fabrics__
DATE OF INITIAL EMPLOYMENT __February 19, 19--__   YEAR __20--__

PAY PERIOD ENDED	VACATION TIME				SICK LEAVE TIME				PERSONAL LEAVE TIME			
	BEGIN. HOURS AVAIL.	HOURS EARNED	HOURS USED	ACC. HOURS AVAIL.	BEGIN. HOURS AVAIL.	HOURS EARNED	HOURS USED	ACC. HOURS AVAIL.	BEGIN. HOURS AVAIL.	HOURS EARNED	HOURS USED	ACC. HOURS AVAIL.
4												
5												
6												
7												
8												
9												

BENEFITS RECORD

EMPLOYEE NO. __3__   EMPLOYEE NAME __Gary M. Evans__   DEPARTMENT __Supplies__
DATE OF INITIAL EMPLOYMENT __November 7, 19--__   YEAR __20--__

PAY PERIOD ENDED	VACATION TIME				SICK LEAVE TIME				PERSONAL LEAVE TIME			
	BEGIN. HOURS AVAIL.	HOURS EARNED	HOURS USED	ACC. HOURS AVAIL.	BEGIN. HOURS AVAIL.	HOURS EARNED	HOURS USED	ACC. HOURS AVAIL.	BEGIN. HOURS AVAIL.	HOURS EARNED	HOURS USED	ACC. HOURS AVAIL.
4												
5												
6												
7												
8												
9												

Name _____ Date _____ Class _____

3-8 MASTERY PROBLEM (continued)

[1]

BENEFITS RECORD

EMPLOYEE NO. 4   EMPLOYEE NAME Marcel P. Ostenbauer   DEPARTMENT Supplies

DATE OF INITIAL EMPLOYMENT June 3, 19--   YEAR 20--

PAY PERIOD ENDED	VACATION TIME				SICK LEAVE TIME				PERSONAL LEAVE TIME			
	BEGIN. HOURS AVAIL.	HOURS EARNED	HOURS USED	ACC. HOURS AVAIL.	BEGIN. HOURS AVAIL.	HOURS EARNED	HOURS USED	ACC. HOURS AVAIL.	BEGIN. HOURS AVAIL.	HOURS EARNED	HOURS USED	ACC. HOURS AVAIL.
4												
5												
6												
7												
8												
9												

BENEFITS RECORD

EMPLOYEE NO. 5   EMPLOYEE NAME Jean R. Quigley   DEPARTMENT Fabrics

DATE OF INITIAL EMPLOYMENT July 9, 19--   YEAR 20--

PAY PERIOD ENDED	VACATION TIME				SICK LEAVE TIME				PERSONAL LEAVE TIME			
	BEGIN. HOURS AVAIL.	HOURS EARNED	HOURS USED	ACC. HOURS AVAIL.	BEGIN. HOURS AVAIL.	HOURS EARNED	HOURS USED	ACC. HOURS AVAIL.	BEGIN. HOURS AVAIL.	HOURS EARNED	HOURS USED	ACC. HOURS AVAIL.
4												
5												
6												
7												
8												
9												

BENEFITS RECORD

EMPLOYEE NO. 6   EMPLOYEE NAME Robert J. Trumpley   DEPARTMENT Administrative

DATE OF INITIAL EMPLOYMENT August 3, 19--   YEAR 20--

PAY PERIOD ENDED	VACATION TIME				SICK LEAVE TIME				PERSONAL LEAVE TIME			
	BEGIN. HOURS AVAIL.	HOURS EARNED	HOURS USED	ACC. HOURS AVAIL.	BEGIN. HOURS AVAIL.	HOURS EARNED	HOURS USED	ACC. HOURS AVAIL.	BEGIN. HOURS AVAIL.	HOURS EARNED	HOURS USED	ACC. HOURS AVAIL.
4												
5												
6												
7												
8												
9												

3-8 MASTERY PROBLEM (continued)

[1-3]

Employee 1: Shanna L. Kim
NAME: Shanna L. Kim
DEPARTMENT: Fabrics
EMPLOYEE NO. 1
PAY PERIOD ENDED 2/13/20--

MORNING		AFTERNOON		OVERTIME		HOURS	
IN	OUT	IN	OUT	IN	OUT	REG	OT
M 8:58	M 11:58	M 1:00	M 6:00	M 7:00	M 8:30		
T 9:00	T 12:01	T 1:00	T 2:01				
W 8:59	W 12:00	W 12:58	W 6:00				
T 9:01	T 12:00	T 1:02	T 6:03				
		F 2:01	F 6:00				
M 8:58	M 12:01	M 1:00	M 6:01				
T 9:00	T 12:00	T 1:00	T 6:02				
W 8:58	W 12:01	W 1:01	W 5:00				
T 9:01	T 12:00	T 1:00	T 6:00	T 7:00	T 8:30		
F 9:00	F 12:02						

	HOURS	RATE	AMOUNT
REGULAR		7.50	
OVERTIME			
TOTAL HOURS		TOTAL EARNINGS	

Employee 3: Gary M. Evans
NAME: Gary M. Evans
DEPARTMENT: Supplies
EMPLOYEE NO. 3
PAY PERIOD ENDED 2/13/20--

MORNING		AFTERNOON		OVERTIME		HOURS	
IN	OUT	IN	OUT	IN	OUT	REG	OT
T 9:00	T 12:01	T 1:00	T 6:00	T 7:00	T 8:30		
W 8:58	W 12:00	W 1:01	W 6:03				
T 9:02	T 12:01						
F 9:00	F 12:00	F 1:00	F 6:01				
		M 1:00	M 6:01				
T 9:00	T 12:03	T 1:01	T 6:00				
W 9:00	W 12:00	W 1:00	W 6:01	W 7:00	W 8:00		
T 9:01	T 12:00	T 1:01	T 6:00				
F 9:00	F 12:00	F 1:02	F 6:00				

	HOURS	RATE	AMOUNT
REGULAR		7.50	
OVERTIME			
TOTAL HOURS		TOTAL EARNINGS	

3-8 MASTERY PROBLEM (continued)

[1-3]

NAME Jean R. Quigley
DEPARTMENT Fabrics
EMPLOYEE NO. 5
PAY PERIOD ENDED 2/13/20--

MORNING		AFTERNOON		OVERTIME		HOURS	
IN	OUT	IN	OUT	IN	OUT	REG	OT
T 9:00	T 12:59	T 2:00	T 6:02	T 7:00	T 8:30		
		W 2:00	W 6:01				
T 8:58	T 1:00	T 2:01	T 6:00				
F 9:01	F 1:02	F 2:00	F 6:03				
S 9:00	S 1:00	S 2:01	S 6:00				
T 9:00	T 1:03	T 2:00	T 6:00	T 7:30	T 9:30		
W 8:58	W 1:00	W 2:01	W 6:01				
T 9:00	T 1:03	T 2:00	T 4:00				

	HOURS	RATE	AMOUNT
REGULAR		6.50	
OVERTIME			
TOTAL HOURS		TOTAL EARNINGS	

NAME Robert J. Trumpley
DEPARTMENT Administrative
EMPLOYEE NO. 6
PAY PERIOD ENDED 2/13/20--

MORNING		AFTERNOON		OVERTIME		HOURS	
IN	OUT	IN	OUT	IN	OUT	REG	OT
T 9:00	T 12:01	T 1:00	T 6:00	T 7:00	T 8:30		
W 8:58	W 12:00	W 1:01	W 6:03				
T 9:02	T 12:01	T 1:00	T 6:00	T 7:30	T 8:30		
F 9:00	F 12:00	F 1:00	F 3:01				
M 9:01	M 12:00	M 1:00	M 6:01				
T 9:00	T 12:03	T 1:01	T 6:00	T 7:00	T 9:00		
W 9:00	W 12:00	W 1:00	W 6:01	W 7:30	W 9:00		
T 9:01	T 12:00	T 1:01	T 2:00				
F 9:00	F 12:00	F 1:02	F 6:00				

	HOURS	RATE	AMOUNT
REGULAR		6.50	
OVERTIME			
TOTAL HOURS		TOTAL EARNINGS	

3-8 MASTERY PROBLEM (continued)

[4]

COMMISSIONS RECORD

EMPLOYEE NO. __2__   EMPLOYEE NAME __Paula D. Brown__

COMMISSION RATE __1.0%__   MONTH __January__   YEAR __20--__

DEPT. __Fabrics__   REGULAR BIWEEKLY SALARY __$600.00__

Sales

    Sales on Account . . . . $ _____

    Cash and Credit Card Sales . . . . _____

    Total Sales . . . . $ _____

    Less: Sales Discounts. . . . . $ _____

        Sales Returns
        and Allowances . . . . _____   _____

    Net Sales. . . . . $ _____

    Commission on Net Sales. . . . . $ _____

COMMISSIONS RECORD

EMPLOYEE NO. __4__   EMPLOYEE NAME __Marcel P. Ostenbauer__

COMMISSION RATE __1.0%__   MONTH __January__   YEAR __20--__

DEPT. __Supplies__   REGULAR BIWEEKLY SALARY __$600.00__

Sales

    Sales on Account . . . . $ _____

    Cash and Credit Card Sales . . . . _____

    Total Sales . . . . $ _____

    Less: Sales Discounts. . . . . $ _____

        Sales Returns
        and Allowances . . . . _____   _____

    Net Sales. . . . . $ _____

    Commission on Net Sales. . . . . $ _____

3-8 MASTERY PROBLEM (continued)

[5]

PAYROLL REGISTER
PAY PERIOD ENDED February 13, 20--

	EMPL. NO.	EMPLOYEE NAME	MARITAL STATUS	NO. OF ALLOWANCES	TOTAL HOURS	EARNINGS REGULAR	OVERTIME	COMMISSION	TOTAL	
1	2	Brown, Paula D.	M	3						1
2	3	Evans, Gary M.	S	2						2
3	1	Kim, Shanna L.	S	1						3
4	4	Ostenbauer, Marcel P.	M	2						4
5	5	Quigley, Jean R.	M	2						5
6	6	Trumpley, Robert J.	S	1						6
7										7
8										8
9										9
10										10
11										11
12										12

[6]

EARNINGS RECORD FOR QUARTER ENDED March 31, 20--

EMPLOYEE NO. 1 NAME Shanna L. Kim SOCIAL SECURITY NO. 213-30-9403
MARITAL STATUS S WITHHOLDING ALLOWANCES 1 HOURLY RATE $7.50 SALARY
DEPARTMENT Fabrics POSITION Salesclerk

PAY PERIOD NO.	ENDED	TOTAL EARNINGS	DEDUCTIONS FEDERAL INCOME TAX	STATE INCOME TAX	SOC. SEC. TAX	MEDICARE TAX	OTHER		TOTAL	NET PAY	ACCUMULATED EARNINGS
3	1/30	600 00	61 00	30 00	39 00	9 00	H L	4 80 / 8 20	162 00	438 00	1833 75
4											
QUARTERLY TOTALS											

3-8 MASTERY PROBLEM (continued)

[5]

PAYROLL REGISTER

DATE OF PAYMENT Feb. 20, 20--

	DEPARTMENT		ADMIN. SALARIES	DEDUCTIONS						PAID	
	FABRIC	SUPPLIES		FEDERAL INCOME TAX	STATE INCOME TAX	SOC. SEC. TAX	MEDICARE TAX	OTHER	TOTAL	NET PAY	CHECK NO.
1											
2											
3											
4											
5											
6											
7											
8											
9											
10											
11											
12											

[6]

EARNINGS RECORD FOR QUARTER ENDED March 31, 20--

EMPLOYEE NO. 2   NAME Paula D. Brown   SOCIAL SECURITY NO. 212-60-3120
MARITAL STATUS M   WITHHOLDING ALLOWANCES 3   HOURLY RATE   SALARY $600.00
DEPARTMENT Fabrics   POSITION Supervisor

PAY PERIOD		TOTAL EARNINGS	DEDUCTIONS						NET PAY	ACCUMULATED EARNINGS
NO.	ENDED		FEDERAL INCOME TAX	STATE INCOME TAX	SOC. SEC. TAX	MEDICARE TAX	OTHER	TOTAL		
3	1/30	600.00	8.00	30.00	39.00	9.00	H 14.80 L 8.20	109.00	491.00	1938.40
4										
QUARTERLY TOTALS										

3-8 MASTERY PROBLEM (continued)

[6]

EARNINGS RECORD FOR QUARTER ENDED March 31, 20--

EMPLOYEE NO. 3 NAME Gary M. Evans SOCIAL SECURITY NO. 162-04-1612
MARITAL STATUS S WITHHOLDING ALLOWANCES 2 HOURLY RATE $7.50 SALARY
DEPARTMENT Supplies POSITION Salesclerk

PAY PERIOD		TOTAL EARNINGS	DEDUCTIONS					TOTAL	NET PAY	ACCUMULATED EARNINGS
NO.	ENDED		FEDERAL INCOME TAX	STATE INCOME TAX	SOC. SEC. TAX	MEDICARE TAX	OTHER			
3	1/30	560 00	40 00	28 00	36 40	8 40	H 4 80 / L 8 20	135 80	424 20	1722 00
4										
QUARTERLY TOTALS										

EARNINGS RECORD FOR QUARTER ENDED March 31, 20--

EMPLOYEE NO. 4 NAME Marcel P. Ostenbauer SOCIAL SECURITY NO. 265-14-3810
MARITAL STATUS M WITHHOLDING ALLOWANCES 2 HOURLY RATE SALARY $600.00
DEPARTMENT Supplies POSITION Supervisor

PAY PERIOD		TOTAL EARNINGS	DEDUCTIONS					TOTAL	NET PAY	ACCUMULATED EARNINGS
NO.	ENDED		FEDERAL INCOME TAX	STATE INCOME TAX	SOC. SEC. TAX	MEDICARE TAX	OTHER			
3	1/30	600 00	24 00	30 00	39 00	9 00	H 4 80 / L 8 20	125 00	475 00	1943 15
4										
QUARTERLY TOTALS										

3-8 MASTERY PROBLEM (continued)

[6]

EARNINGS RECORD FOR QUARTER ENDED March 31, 20--

EMPLOYEE NO. 5 NAME Jean R. Quigley SOCIAL SECURITY NO. 196-36-4402
MARITAL STATUS M WITHHOLDING ALLOWANCES 2 HOURLY RATE $6.50 SALARY
DEPARTMENT Fabrics POSITION Salesclerk

PAY PERIOD		TOTAL EARNINGS	DEDUCTIONS						NET PAY	ACCUMULATED EARNINGS
NO.	ENDED		FEDERAL INCOME TAX	STATE INCOME TAX	SOC. SEC. TAX	MEDICARE TAX	OTHER	TOTAL		
3	1/30	520 00	12 00	26 00	33 80	7 80	H 14 80 / L 8 20	102 60	417 40	1599 00
4										
QUARTERLY TOTALS										

EARNINGS RECORD FOR QUARTER ENDED March 31, 20--

EMPLOYEE NO. 6 NAME Robert J. Trumpley SOCIAL SECURITY NO. 262-36-3136
MARITAL STATUS S WITHHOLDING ALLOWANCES 1 HOURLY RATE $6.50 SALARY
DEPARTMENT Administrative POSITION Clerk

PAY PERIOD		TOTAL EARNINGS	DEDUCTIONS						NET PAY	ACCUMULATED EARNINGS
NO.	ENDED		FEDERAL INCOME TAX	STATE INCOME TAX	SOC. SEC. TAX	MEDICARE TAX	OTHER	TOTAL		
3	1/30	520 00	49 00	26 00	33 80	7 80	H 14 80 / L 8 20	131 80	388 20	1608 75
4										
QUARTERLY TOTALS										

3-8 MASTERY PROBLEM (concluded)

[7]

CASH PAYMENTS JOURNAL PAGE 4

DATE	ACCOUNT TITLE	CK. NO.	POST. REF.	GENERAL DEBIT	GENERAL CREDIT	ACCOUNTS PAYABLE DEBIT	PURCH. DISCOUNT CR. FABRIC	PURCH. DISCOUNT CR. SUPPLIES	CASH CREDIT

[8]

GENERAL JOURNAL PAGE 4

DATE	ACCOUNT TITLE	DOC. NO.	POST. REF.	DEBIT	CREDIT

3-9 CHALLENGE PROBLEM, p. 90

Preparing a benefits record

BENEFITS RECORD

EMPLOYEE NO. 7   EMPLOYEE NAME Arthur J. Delgado   DEPARTMENT Men's Shoes

DATE OF INITIAL EMPLOYMENT June 5, 1986   YEAR 20--

	1	2	3	4	5	6	7	8	9	10	11	12
PAY PERIOD ENDED	VACATION TIME				SICK LEAVE TIME				PERSONAL LEAVE TIME			
	BEGIN. HOURS AVAIL.	HOURS EARNED	HOURS USED	ACC. HOURS AVAIL.	BEGIN. HOURS AVAIL.	HOURS EARNED	HOURS USED	ACC. HOURS AVAIL.	BEGIN. HOURS AVAIL.	HOURS EARNED	HOURS USED	ACC. HOURS AVAIL.
1												
2												
3												
4												
5												
6												
7												
8												
9												
10												
11												
12												
13												

Extra form

BENEFITS RECORD

EMPLOYEE NO. _____   EMPLOYEE NAME _____   DEPARTMENT _____

DATE OF INITIAL EMPLOYMENT _____   YEAR _____

	1	2	3	4	5	6	7	8	9	10	11	12
PAY PERIOD ENDED	VACATION TIME				SICK LEAVE TIME				PERSONAL LEAVE TIME			
	BEGIN. HOURS AVAIL.	HOURS EARNED	HOURS USED	ACC. HOURS AVAIL.	BEGIN. HOURS AVAIL.	HOURS EARNED	HOURS USED	ACC. HOURS AVAIL.	BEGIN. HOURS AVAIL.	HOURS EARNED	HOURS USED	ACC. HOURS AVAIL.
1												
2												
3												
4												
5												
6												
7												
8												
9												
10												
11												
12												
13												
14												
15												
16												

Name _____ Date _____ Class _____

3-9 CHALLENGE PROBLEM

Extra forms

BENEFITS RECORD

EMPLOYEE NO. _____ EMPLOYEE NAME _____ DEPARTMENT _____

DATE OF INITIAL EMPLOYMENT _____ YEAR _____

	1	2	3	4	5	6	7	8	9	10	11	12
PAY PERIOD ENDED	VACATION TIME				SICK LEAVE TIME				PERSONAL LEAVE TIME			
	BEGIN. HOURS AVAIL.	HOURS EARNED	HOURS USED	ACC. HOURS AVAIL.	BEGIN. HOURS AVAIL.	HOURS EARNED	HOURS USED	ACC. HOURS AVAIL.	BEGIN. HOURS AVAIL.	HOURS EARNED	HOURS USED	ACC. HOURS AVAIL.
1												
2												
3												
4												
5												
6												
7												
8												
9												
10												
11												
12												
13												
14												
15												
16												

BENEFITS RECORD

EMPLOYEE NO. _____ EMPLOYEE NAME _____ DEPARTMENT _____

DATE OF INITIAL EMPLOYMENT _____ YEAR _____

	1	2	3	4	5	6	7	8	9	10	11	12
PAY PERIOD ENDED	VACATION TIME				SICK LEAVE TIME				PERSONAL LEAVE TIME			
	BEGIN. HOURS AVAIL.	HOURS EARNED	HOURS USED	ACC. HOURS AVAIL.	BEGIN. HOURS AVAIL.	HOURS EARNED	HOURS USED	ACC. HOURS AVAIL.	BEGIN. HOURS AVAIL.	HOURS EARNED	HOURS USED	ACC. HOURS AVAIL.
1												
2												
3												
4												
5												
6												
7												
8												
9												
10												
11												
12												
13												
14												
15												
16												

Name _____ Date _____ Class _____

4-1 WORK TOGETHER, p. 100

Preparing an interim departmental statement of gross profit [4]

ESTIMATED MERCHANDISE INVENTORY SHEET
Gross Profit Method

DEPARTMENT _____ DATE _____

1	Beginning inventory, January 1...		$_____
2	Net purchases to date		_____
3	Merchandise available for sale..		$_____
4	Net sales to date..	$_____	
5	Less estimated gross profit	_____	
	(Net sales × Estimated gross profit _____%)		
6	Estimated cost of merchandise sold		_____
7	Estimated ending inventory...		$_____

ESTIMATED MERCHANDISE INVENTORY SHEET
Gross Profit Method

DEPARTMENT _____ DATE _____

1	Beginning inventory, January 1...		$_____
2	Net purchases to date		_____
3	Merchandise available for sale..		$_____
4	Net sales to date..	$_____	
5	Less estimated gross profit	_____	
	(Net sales × Estimated gross profit _____%)		
6	Estimated cost of merchandise sold		_____
7	Estimated ending inventory...		$_____

4-1 WORK TOGETHER (concluded)

Willow Glen Interior Design
Interim Departmental Statement of Gross Profit
For Month Ended May 31, 20--

	KITCHEN	% OF NET SALES	BATH	% OF NET SALES	TOTAL	% OF NET SALES
Operating Revenue:						
Net Sales						
Cost of Merchandise Sold:						
Est. Mdse. Inventory, May 1						
Net Purchases						
Mdse. Available for Sale						
Less Est. End. Inv., May 31						
Cost of Merchandise Sold						
Gross Profit on Operations						

4-1 ON YOUR OWN, p. 100

Preparing an interim departmental statement of gross profit [6]

ESTIMATED MERCHANDISE INVENTORY SHEET
Gross Profit Method

DEPARTMENT _____   DATE _____

1	Beginning inventory, January 1...	$_____
2	Net purchases to date	_____
3	Merchandise available for sale..	$_____
4	Net sales to date.. $_____	
5	Less estimated gross profit .... _____	
	(Net sales × Estimated gross profit _____%)	
6	Estimated cost of merchandise sold..	_____
7	Estimated ending inventory...	$_____

ESTIMATED MERCHANDISE INVENTORY SHEET
Gross Profit Method

DEPARTMENT _____   DATE _____

1	Beginning inventory, January 1...	$_____
2	Net purchases to date	_____
3	Merchandise available for sale..	$_____
4	Net sales to date.. $_____	
5	Less estimated gross profit .... _____	
	(Net sales × Estimated gross profit _____%)	
6	Estimated cost of merchandise sold..	_____
7	Estimated ending inventory...	$_____

4-1 ON YOUR OWN (concluded)

[7]

Lassen Heating and Air Conditioning, Inc.
Interim Departmental Statement of Gross Profit
For Month Ended April 30, 20--

	COMMERCIAL	% OF NET SALES	RESIDENTIAL	% OF NET SALES	TOTAL	% OF NET SALES
Operating Revenue:						
Net Sales						
Cost of Merchandise Sold:						
Est. Mdse. Inv., April 1						
Net Purchases						
Mdse. Available for Sale						
Less Est. End. Inv., April 30						
Cost of Merchandise Sold						
Gross Profit on Operations						

4-2 WORK TOGETHER, p. 111

Analyzing adjusting entries [4]

Allowance for Uncollectible Accounts		Federal Income Tax Payable
	Bal. 450.00	

Merchandise Inventory—Stereos		Income Summary—Stereos
Bal. 56,120.00		

Merchandise Inventory—Accessories		Income Summary—Accessories
Bal. 9,590.00		

Federal Income Tax Expense		Uncollectible Accounts Expense
Bal. 12,000.00		

4-2 WORK TOGETHER

Extra form

4-2 ON YOUR OWN, p. 111

Analyzing adjusting entries [5]

Allowance for Uncollectible Accounts	Income Summary—Washers
Bal. 370.00	

Merchandise Inventory—Washers	Income Summary—Dryers
Bal. 83,670.00	

Merchandise Inventory—Dryers	Depreciation Expense—Equipment
Bal. 68,560.00	

Accumulated Depreciation—Equipment	Uncollectible Accounts Expense
Bal. 2,300.00	

Name _____ Date _____ Class _____

4-2 ON YOUR OWN

Extra form

4-3 WORK TOGETHER, p. 118

Preparing an income statement with component percentages

(Note: The partial work sheet is also needed to complete Work Together 4-4.)

Video Scene
Partial Work Sheet
For Year Ended December 31, 20--

	ACCOUNT TITLE	INCOME STATEMENT DEBIT	INCOME STATEMENT CREDIT
31	Income Summary—CDs	9 460 00	
32	Income Summary—Videos		26 090 00
33	Income Summary—General		
34	Sales—CDs		113 640 00
35	Sales—Videos		144 730 00
36	Sales Ret. and Allow.—CDs	3 210 00	
37	Sales Ret. and Allow.—Videos	4 120 00	
38	Purchases—CDs	45 082 00	
39	Purchases—Videos	80 570 00	
40	Purchases Discounts—CDs		1 640 00
41	Purchases Discounts—Videos		2 150 00
42	Purchases Ret. and Allow.—CDs		1 000 00
43	Purchases Ret. and Allow.—Videos		2 000 00
44	Advertising Expense	12 650 00	
45	Depr. Expense—Store Equip.	6 040 00	
46	Supplies Expense—Store	5 823 00	
47	Insurance Expense	8 400 00	
48	Rent Expense	44 000 00	
49	Uncollectible Accounts Expense	2 990 00	
50	Federal Income Tax Expense	12 226 00	
51		234 571 00	291 250 00
52	Net Income after Fed. Inc. Tax	56 679 00	
53		291 250 00	291 250 00
54			

4-3 WORK TOGETHER (continued)

Video Scene
Departmental Statement of Gross Profit
For Year Ended December 31, 20--

	CDs	% OF NET SALES	VIDEOS		% OF NET SALES	TOTAL		% OF NET SALES
Operating Revenue:								
Net Sales		$110,430.00	100.0		$140,610.00	100.0		$251,040.00	100.0
Cost of Merchandise Sold:								
Est. Mdse. Inv., Jan. 1	$ 38,910.00		$ 42,100.00			$ 81,010.00		
Net Purchases	42,442.00		76,420.00			118,862.00		
Mdse. Available for Sale	$ 81,352.00		$118,520.00			$199,872.00		
Less Est. End. Inv., December 31	29,450.00		68,190.00			97,640.00		
Cost of Merchandise Sold		51,902.00	47.0		50,330.00	35.8		102,232.00	40.7
Gross Profit on Operations		$ 58,528.00	53.0		$ 90,280.00	64.2		$148,808.00	59.3

4-3 WORK TOGETHER (concluded)

[4]

Video Scene
Income Statement
For Year Ended December 31, 20--

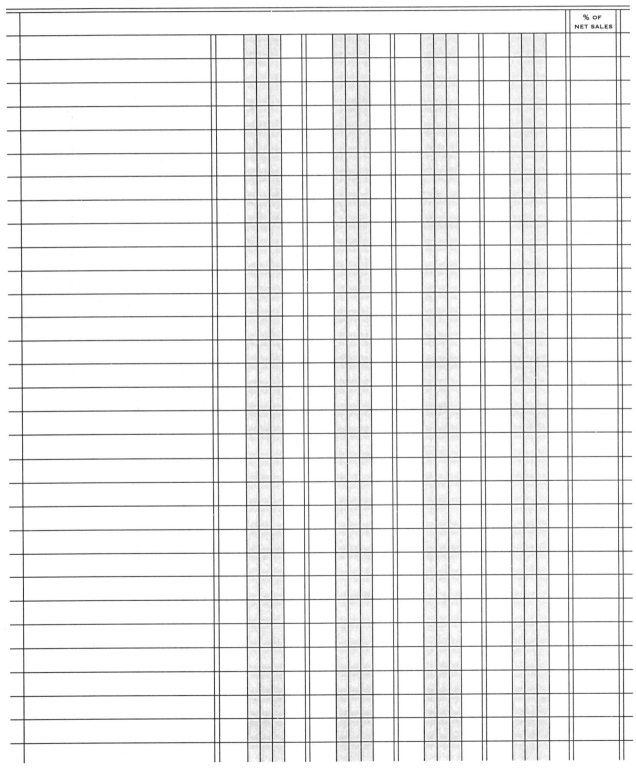

4-3 WORK TOGETHER

Extra form

								% OF NET SALES

4-3 ON YOUR OWN, p. 118

Preparing an income statement with component percentages

(Note: The partial work sheet is also needed to complete On Your Own 4-4.)

Fremont Sign
Partial Work Sheet
For Year Ended December 31, 20--

	ACCOUNT TITLE	INCOME STATEMENT DEBIT	INCOME STATEMENT CREDIT
31	Income Summary—Commercial		4 230 00
32	Income Summary—Residential		24 915 00
33	Income Summary—General		
34	Sales—Commercial		162 700 00
35	Sales—Residential		81 900 00
36	Sales Discounts—Commercial	8 500 00	
37	Sales Discounts—Residential	3 100 00	
38	Purchases—Commercial	74 530 00	
39	Purchases—Residential	55 555 00	
40	Purchases Discounts—Commercial		1 870 00
41	Purchases Discounts—Residential		715 00
42	Purchases Ret. and Allow.—Commercial		630 00
43	Purchases Ret. and Allow.—Residential		840 00
44	Depr. Expense—Shop Equipment	21 300 00	
45	Salary Expense—Commercial	36 720 00	
46	Salary Expense—Residential	30 100 00	
47	Payroll Taxes Expense	9 870 00	
48	Rent Expense	8 200 00	
49	Salary Expense—Admin.	29 000 00	
50	Federal Inc. Tax Expense	139 00	
51		277 014 00	277 800 00
52	Net Income after Fed. Inc. Tax	786 00	
53		277 800 00	277 800 00
54			

4-3 ON YOUR OWN (continued)

Fremont Sign
Departmental Statement of Gross Profit
For Year Ended December 31, 20--

	COMMERCIAL		% OF NET SALES	RESIDENTIAL		% OF NET SALES	TOTAL		% OF NET SALES
Operating Revenue:									
Net Sales		$154,200.00	100.0		$ 78,800.00	100.0		$233,000.00	100.0
Cost of Merchandise Sold:									
Est. Mdse. Inv., Jan. 1	$ 18,710.00			$ 12,715.00			$ 31,425.00		
Net Purchases	72,030.00			54,000.00			126,030.00		
Mdse. Available for Sale	$ 90,740.00			$ 66,715.00			$157,455.00		
Less Est. End. Inv., Dec. 31	22,940.00			37,630.00			60,570.00		
Cost of Merchandise Sold		67,800.00	44.0		29,085.00	36.9		96,885.00	41.6
Gross Profit on Operations		$ 86,400.00	56.0		$ 49,715.00	63.1		$136,115.00	58.4

4-3 ON YOUR OWN (concluded)

[5]

Fremont Sign
Income Statement
For Year Ended December 31, 20--

						% OF NET SALES

4-3 ON YOUR OWN

Extra form

							% OF NET SALES

4-4 WORK TOGETHER, p. 124

Journalizing closing entries [5]

Use the income statement columns of Video Scene's work sheet on page 103.

GENERAL JOURNAL   PAGE 4

DATE	ACCOUNT TITLE	DOC. NO.	POST. REF.	DEBIT	CREDIT

4-4 WORK TOGETHER

Extra form

GENERAL JOURNAL

PAGE _____

	DATE	ACCOUNT TITLE	DOC. NO.	POST. REF.	DEBIT	CREDIT	
1							1
2							2
3							3
4							4
5							5
6							6
7							7
8							8
9							9
10							10
11							11
12							12
13							13
14							14
15							15
16							16
17							17
18							18
19							19
20							20
21							21
22							22
23							23
24							24
25							25
26							26
27							27
28							28
29							29
30							30
31							31

Working Papers

COPYRIGHT © SOUTH-WESTERN EDUCATIONAL PUBLISHING

4-4 ON YOUR OWN, p. 124

Journalizing closing entries [6]

Use the income statement columns of Fremont Sign's work sheet on page 107.

GENERAL JOURNAL — PAGE 6

	DATE	ACCOUNT TITLE	DOC. NO.	POST. REF.	DEBIT	CREDIT	
1							1
2							2
3							3
4							4
5							5
6							6
7							7
8							8
9							9
10							10
11							11
12							12
13							13
14							14
15							15
16							16
17							17
18							18
19							19
20							20
21							21
22							22
23							23
24							24
25							25
26							26
27							27
28							28
29							29
30							30

Name _____ Date _____ Class _____

4-4 ON YOUR OWN

Extra form

GENERAL JOURNAL PAGE ____

	DATE	ACCOUNT TITLE	DOC. NO.	POST. REF.	DEBIT	CREDIT	
1							1
2							2
3							3
4							4
5							5
6							6
7							7
8							8
9							9
10							10
11							11
12							12
13							13
14							14
15							15
16							16
17							17
18							18
19							19
20							20
21							21
22							22
23							23
24							24
25							25
26							26
27							27
28							28
29							29
30							30
31							31

4-1 APPLICATION PROBLEM, p. 126

Estimating ending merchandise inventory

ESTIMATED MERCHANDISE INVENTORY SHEET
Gross Profit Method

DEPARTMENT _____ DATE _____

1. Beginning inventory, January 1.. $ _____
2. Net purchases to date .... _____
3. Merchandise available for sale....................................... $ _____
4. Net sales to date................................... $ _____
5. Less estimated gross profit .... _____
   (Net sales × Estimated gross profit _____%)
6. Estimated cost of merchandise sold.................................. _____
7. Estimated ending inventory... $ _____

ESTIMATED MERCHANDISE INVENTORY SHEET
Gross Profit Method

DEPARTMENT _____ DATE _____

1. Beginning inventory, January 1.. $ _____
2. Net purchases to date .... _____
3. Merchandise available for sale....................................... $ _____
4. Net sales to date................................... $ _____
5. Less estimated gross profit .... _____
   (Net sales × Estimated gross profit _____%)
6. Estimated cost of merchandise sold.................................. _____
7. Estimated ending inventory... $ _____

Name _____ Date _____ Class _____

4-1 APPLICATION PROBLEM

Extra forms

ESTIMATED MERCHANDISE INVENTORY SHEET
Gross Profit Method

DEPARTMENT _____ DATE _____

1	Beginning inventory, January 1...	$ _____
2	Net purchases to date	_____
3	Merchandise available for sale..	$ _____
4	Net sales to date... $ _____	
5	Less estimated gross profit .... _____	
	(Net sales × Estimated gross profit _____%)	
6	Estimated cost of merchandise sold...	_____
7	Estimated ending inventory..	$ _____

ESTIMATED MERCHANDISE INVENTORY SHEET
Gross Profit Method

DEPARTMENT _____ DATE _____

1	Beginning inventory, January 1...	$ _____
2	Net purchases to date	_____
3	Merchandise available for sale..	$ _____
4	Net sales to date... $ _____	
5	Less estimated gross profit .... _____	
	(Net sales × Estimated gross profit _____%)	
6	Estimated cost of merchandise sold...	_____
7	Estimated ending inventory..	$ _____

4-2 APPLICATION PROBLEM, p. 126

Preparing an interim departmental statement of gross profit, calculating component percentages [1]

ESTIMATED MERCHANDISE INVENTORY SHEET
Gross Profit Method

DEPARTMENT _____ DATE _____

1	Beginning inventory, January 1	$ _____
2	Net purchases to date	_____
3	Merchandise available for sale	$ _____
4	Net sales to date .... $ _____	
5	Less estimated gross profit .... _____	
	(Net sales × Estimated gross profit _____%)	
6	Estimated cost of merchandise sold	_____
7	Estimated ending inventory	$ _____

ESTIMATED MERCHANDISE INVENTORY SHEET
Gross Profit Method

DEPARTMENT _____ DATE _____

1	Beginning inventory, January 1	$ _____
2	Net purchases to date	_____
3	Merchandise available for sale	$ _____
4	Net sales to date .... $ _____	
5	Less estimated gross profit .... _____	
	(Net sales × Estimated gross profit _____%)	
6	Estimated cost of merchandise sold	_____
7	Estimated ending inventory	$ _____

4-2 APPLICATION PROBLEM (concluded)

[2]

Allied Lighting
Interim Departmental Statement of Gross Profit
For Month Ended March 31, 20--

	OFFICE	% OF NET SALES	RESIDENTIAL	% OF NET SALES	TOTAL	% OF NET SALES
Operating Revenue:						
Net Sales						
Cost of Merchandise Sold:						
Est. Mdse. Inv., March 1						
Net Purchases						
Mdse. Available for Sale						
Less Est. End. Inv., March 31						
Cost of Merchandise Sold						
Gross Profit on Operations						

4-3 APPLICATION PROBLEM, p. 126

Preparing subsidiary schedules [1]

Gabriel's Gourmet Shop

Schedule of Accounts Payable

December 31, 20--

[2]

Gabriel's Gourmet Shop

Schedule of Accounts Receivable

December 31, 20--

Name _____ Date _____ Class _____

4-3 APPLICATION PROBLEM

Extra forms

4-4 APPLICATION PROBLEM, p. 127

Calculating and analyzing component percentage for total operating expenses [1, 2]

1	2	3	4	5	6
Business	Net Sales	Total Operating Expenses	Performance Standard—Not more than	Component Percentage	Performance Level
1	$148,000.00	$43,500.00	32.0%	29.4%	A
2	$175,500.00	$51,750.00	30.0%		
3	$130,300.00	$36,500.00	26.0%		
4	$145,600.00	$35,930.00	25.0%		
5	$185,300.00	$58,250.00	30.0%		
6	$163,900.00	$44,980.00	28.0%		

Extra form

1	2	3	4	5	6
Business	Net Sales	Total Operating Expenses	Performance Standard—Not more than	Component Percentage	Performance Level

Name _____ Date _____ Class _____

4-4 APPLICATION PROBLEM

Extra forms

1 Business	2 Net Sales	3 Total Operating Expenses	4 Performance Standard—Not more than	5 Component Percentage	6 Performance Level

1 Business	2 Net Sales	3 Total Operating Expenses	4 Performance Standard—Not more than	5 Component Percentage	6 Performance Level

4-5 APPLICATION PROBLEM

(Note: Work sheet for Application Problem 4-5 begins on page 124.)

Extra form

4-5 APPLICATION PROBLEM, page 128

Completing a work sheet for a departmentalized business

Note: This work sheet is needed to complete Application Problems 4-6 and 4-7.

Regis Bookstore
Work Sheet
For Year Ended December 31, 20--

	ACCOUNT TITLE	TRIAL BALANCE DEBIT	TRIAL BALANCE CREDIT	ADJUSTMENTS DEBIT	ADJUSTMENTS CREDIT	INCOME STATEMENT DEBIT	INCOME STATEMENT CREDIT	BALANCE SHEET DEBIT	BALANCE SHEET CREDIT
1	Cash	3760068							
2	Petty Cash	50000							
3	Accounts Receivable	2094860							
4	Allowance for Uncollectible Accounts		32080						
5	Mdse. Inventory—Teens	17896030							
6	Mdse. Inventory—Adults	16038040							
7	Supplies—Office	1094000							
8	Supplies—Store	962060							
9	Prepaid Insurance	880000							
10	Office Equipment	1890000							
11	Accum. Depr.—Office Equipment		884000						
12	Store Equipment	2160000							
13	Accum. Depr.—Store Equipment		1031000						
14	Accounts Payable		2998030						
15	Employee Income Tax Pay.—Federal		132040						
16	Employee Income Tax Pay.—State		86010						
17	Federal Income Tax Payable								
18	Social Security Tax Payable		170950						
19	Medicare Tax Payable		39450						
20	Sales Tax Payable		683040						
21	Unemploy. Tax Pay.—Federal		1930						
22	Unemploy. Tax Pay.—State		13028						
23	Health Ins. Prem. Payable		299000						
24	Dividends Payable								
25	Capital Stock		20000000						
26	Dividends	3000000							
27	Retained Earnings		15567500						
28	Income Summary—Teens								
29	Income Summary—Adults								
30	Income Summary—General								

4-5 APPLICATION PROBLEM (concluded)

	ACCOUNT TITLE	TRIAL BALANCE		ADJUSTMENTS		INCOME STATEMENT		BALANCE SHEET	
		DEBIT	CREDIT	DEBIT	CREDIT	DEBIT	CREDIT	DEBIT	CREDIT
31	Sales—Teens		38716980						
32	Sales—Adults		33789470						
33	Sales Discount—Teens	361080							
34	Sales Discount—Adults	379010							
35	Sales Ret. & Allow.—Teens	231080							
36	Sales Ret. & Allow.—Adults	294060							
37	Purchases—Teens	20221190							
38	Purchases—Adults	19694150							
39	Purchases Discount—Teens		513080						
40	Purchases Discount—Adults		473020						
41	Purch. Ret. & Allow.—Teens		396030						
42	Purch. Ret. & Allow.—Adults		428070						
43	Advertising Expense	548000							
44	Credit Card Fee Expense	476080							
45	Depr. Exp.—Store Equipment								
46	Salary Expense—Teens	7280000							
47	Salary Expense—Adults	7630000							
48	Supplies Expense—Store								
49	Depr. Exp.—Office Equipment								
50	Insurance Expense								
51	Miscellaneous Expense	463000							
52	Payroll Taxes Expense	1834000							
53	Rent Expense	1800000							
54	Salary Expense—Administrative	3986000							
55	Supplies Expense—Office								
56	Uncollectible Accounts Expense								
57	Federal Income Tax Expense	1232000							
58		116254708	116254708						
59									
60									

4-5 APPLICATION PROBLEM

Extra form

4-6 APPLICATION PROBLEM, p. 128

Preparing financial statements for a departmentalized business [1]

Note: The work sheet from Application Problem 4-5 is needed to complete this problem.

Regis Bookstore
Departmental Statement of Gross Profit
For Year Ended December 31, 20--

	TEENS	% OF NET SALES	ADULTS	% OF NET SALES	TOTAL	% OF NET SALES
Operating Revenue:						
Net Sales						
Cost of Merchandise Sold:						
Mdse. Inv., Jan. 1						
Net Purchases						
Mdse. Available for Sale						
Less End. Inv., Dec. 31						
Cost of Merchandise Sold						
Gross Profit on Operations						

4-6 APPLICATION PROBLEM (continued)

[2]

Regis Bookstore
Income Statement
For Year Ended December 31, 20--

						% OF NET SALES
Operating Revenue:						
Sales:						
Less: Sales Discount						
Sales Returns & Allow.						
Net Sales						
Cost of Merchandise Sold:						
Mdse. Inv., Jan. 1, 20--						
Purchases						
Less: Purchases Discount						
Purch. Returns & Allow.						
Net Purchases						
Total Cost of Mdse. Avail. for Sale						
Less Mdse. Inv., Dec. 31, 20--						
Cost of Merchandise Sold						
Gross Profit on Operations						
Operating Expenses:						
Selling Expenses:						
Advertising Expense						
Credit Card Fee Expense						
Depr. Exp.—Store Equipment						
Salary Expense—Teens						
Salary Expense—Adults						
Supplies Expense—Store						
Total Selling Expenses						
Administrative Expenses:						
Depr. Exp.—Office Equipment						
Insurance Expense						
Miscellaneous Expense						
Payroll Taxes Expense						
Rent Expense						
Salary Expense—Administrative						

4-6 APPLICATION PROBLEM (continued)

[2]

Regis Bookstore
Income Statement (continued)
For Year Ended December 31, 20--

													% OF NET SALES
Supplies Expense—Office													
Uncollectible Accounts Expense													
Total Administrative Expenses													
Total Operating Expenses													
Net Income before Fed. Inc. Tax													
Less Federal Income Tax Expense													
Net Income after Fed. Inc. Tax													

4-6 APPLICATION PROBLEM (continued)

[3]

Regis Bookstore
Statement of Stockholders' Equity
For Year Ended December 31, 20--

Capital Stock:			
Per Share			
January 1, 20--, Shares Issued			
Issued during Current Year,			
Balance, December 31, 20--, Shares Issued			
Retained Earnings:			
Balance, January 1, 20--			
Net Income after Federal Income Tax for 20--			
Less Dividends Declared during 20--			
Net Increase during 20--			
Balance, December 31, 20--			
Total Stockholders' Equity, December 31, 20--			

4-6 APPLICATION PROBLEM (continued)

[4]

Regis Bookstore
Balance Sheet
December 31, 20--

Assets						
Current Assets:						
Cash						
Petty Cash						
Accounts Receivable						
Less Allowance for Uncollectible Accounts						
Merchandise Inventory—Teens						
Merchandise Inventory—Adults						
Supplies—Office						
Supplies—Store						
Prepaid Insurance						
Total Current Assets						
Plant Assets:						
Office Equipment						
Less Accumulated Depr.—Office Equipment						
Store Equipment						
Less Accumulated Depr.—Store Equipment						
Total Plant Assets						
Total Assets						
Liabilities						
Current Liabilities:						
Accounts Payable						
Employee Income Tax Payable—Federal						
Employee Income Tax Payable—State						
Federal Income Tax Payable						
Social Security Tax Payable						
Medicare Tax Payable						
Sales Tax Payable						
Unemployment Tax Payable—Federal						
Unemployment Tax Payable—State						
Health Insurance Premiums Payable						
Total Liabilities						

4-6 APPLICATION PROBLEM (concluded)

[4]

Regis Bookstore
Balance Sheet (continued)
December 31, 20--

Stockholders' Equity				
Capital Stock				
Retained Earnings				
Total Stockholders' Equity				
Total Liabilities & Stockholders' Equity				

4-7 APPLICATION PROBLEM, p. 129

Journalizing adjusting and closing entries for a departmentalized business [1, 2]

Note: The work sheet from Application Problem 4-5 is needed to complete this problem.

GENERAL JOURNAL   PAGE 15

	DATE	ACCOUNT TITLE	DOC. NO.	POST. REF.	DEBIT	CREDIT	
1							1
2							2
3							3
4							4
5							5
6							6
7							7
8							8
9							9
10							10
11							11
12							12
13							13
14							14
15							15
16							16
17							17
18							18
19							19
20							20
21							21
22							22
23							23
24							24
25							25
26							26
27							27
28							28
29							29
30							30

4-7 APPLICATION PROBLEM (continued)

[2]

GENERAL JOURNAL PAGE 16

DATE	ACCOUNT TITLE	DOC. NO.	POST. REF.	DEBIT	CREDIT

4-8 MASTERY PROBLEM, p. 129

(Note: The work sheet for this problem begins on page 136.)

Preparing end-of-fiscal-period work for a departmentalized business [2]

Home Plate Sporting Goods
Departmental Statement of Gross Profit
For Year Ended December 31, 20--

	SOFTBALL	% OF NET SALES	BASEBALL	% OF NET SALES	TOTAL	% OF NET SALES
Operating Revenue:						
Net Sales						
Cost of Merchandise Sold:						
Mdse. Inv., Jan. 1						
Net Purchases						
Mdse. Available for Sale						
Less End. Inv., Dec. 31						
Cost of Merchandise Sold						
Gross Profit on Operations						

4-8 MASTERY PROBLEM (continued)

[1]

Home Plate Sporting Goods
Work Sheet
For Year Ended December 31, 20--

	ACCOUNT TITLE	TRIAL BALANCE DEBIT	TRIAL BALANCE CREDIT	ADJUSTMENTS DEBIT	ADJUSTMENTS CREDIT	INCOME STATEMENT DEBIT	INCOME STATEMENT CREDIT	BALANCE SHEET DEBIT	BALANCE SHEET CREDIT	
1	Cash	38 560 40								1
2	Petty Cash	600 00								2
3	Accounts Receivable	26 364 20								3
4	Allowance for Uncollectible Accounts		46 80							4
5	Mdse. Inventory—Softball	220 180 00								5
6	Mdse. Inventory—Baseball	247 240 00								6
7	Supplies—Office	1 444 00								7
8	Supplies—Store	948 360								8
9	Prepaid Insurance	8 550 00								9
10	Office Equipment	17 940 00								10
11	Accum. Depr.—Office Equipment		9 360 00							11
12	Store Equipment	22 860 00								12
13	Accum. Depr.—Store Equipment		11 430 00							13
14	Accounts Payable		32 740 00							14
15	Employee Income Tax Pay.—Federal		1 340 90							15
16	Employee Income Tax Pay.—State		930 60							16
17	Federal Income Tax Payable									17
18	Social Security Tax Payable		1 917 50							18
19	Medicare Tax Payable		442 50							19
20	Sales Tax Payable		7 240 30							20
21	Unemploy. Tax Pay.—Federal		22 40							21
22	Unemploy. Tax Pay.—State		151 20							22
23	Health Ins. Prem. Payable		354 00							23
24	Dividends Payable									24
25	Capital Stock		300 000 00							25
26	Dividends	30 000 00								26
27	Retained Earnings		155 000 00							27
28	Income Summary—Softball									28
29	Income Summary—Baseball									29
30	Income Summary—General									30

4-8 MASTERY PROBLEM (continued)

[1]

	ACCOUNT TITLE	TRIAL BALANCE		ADJUSTMENTS		INCOME STATEMENT		BALANCE SHEET	
		DEBIT	CREDIT	DEBIT	CREDIT	DEBIT	CREDIT	DEBIT	CREDIT
31	Sales—Softball		386 93 0 30						
32	Sales—Baseball		366 80 0 80						
33	Sales Discount—Softball	2 86 0 00							
34	Sales Discount—Baseball	2 43 0 80							
35	Sales Ret. & Allow.—Softball	2 64 0 30							
36	Sales Ret. & Allow.—Baseball	3 21 0 00							
37	Purchases—Softball	201 08 6 90							
38	Purchases—Baseball	188 09 8 00							
39	Purchases Discount—Softball		3 39 0 10						
40	Purchases Discount—Baseball		3 63 0 00						
41	Purch. Ret. & Allow.—Softball		4 21 0 80						
42	Purch. Ret. & Allow.—Baseball		3 96 0 00						
43	Advertising Expense	5 73 0 00							
44	Credit Card Fee Expense	5 16 0 00							
45	Depr. Exp.—Store Equipment								
46	Salary Expense—Softball	68 30 0 00							
47	Salary Expense—Baseball	72 50 0 00							
48	Supplies Expense—Store								
49	Depr. Exp.—Office Equipment								
50	Insurance Expense								
51	Miscellaneous Expense	4 86 0 00							
52	Payroll Taxes Expense	25 60 4 00							
53	Rent Expense	21 60 0 00							
54	Salary Expense—Administrative	41 30 0 00							
55	Supplies Expense—Office								
56	Uncollectible Accounts Expense								
57	Federal Income Tax Expense	11 90 0 00							
58		1293 49 8 20	1293 49 8 20						
59									
60									

4-8 MASTERY PROBLEM (continued)

[3]

Home Plate Sporting Goods
Income Statement
For Year Ended December 31, 20--

						% OF NET SALES
Operating Revenue:						
Sales:						
Less: Sales Discount						
Sales Returns & Allow.						
Net Sales						
Cost of Merchandise Sold:						
Mdse. Inv., Jan. 1, 20--						
Purchases						
Less: Purchases Discount						
Purch. Returns & Allow.						
Net Purchases						
Total Cost of Mdse. Available						
Less Mdse. Inv., Dec. 31, 20--						
Cost of Merchandise Sold						
Gross Profit on Operations						
Operating Expenses:						
Selling Expenses:						
Advertising Expense						
Credit Card Fee Expense						
Depr. Exp.—Store Equipment						
Salary Expense—Softball						
Salary Expense—Baseball						
Supplies Expense—Store						
Total Selling Expenses						
Administrative Expenses:						
Depr. Exp.—Office Equipment						
Insurance Expense						
Miscellaneous Expense						
Payroll Taxes Expense						
Rent Expense						
Salary Expense—Administrative						

4-8 MASTERY PROBLEM (continued)

[3]

Home Plate Sporting Goods

Income Statement (continued)

For Year Ended December 31, 20--

					% OF NET SALES
Supplies Expense—Office					
Uncollectible Accounts Expense					
Total Administrative Expenses					
Total Operating Expenses					
Net Income before Fed. Inc. Tax					
Less Federal Income Tax Expense					
Net Income after Fed. Inc. Tax					

[4]

Home Plate Sporting Goods

Statement of Stockholders' Equity

For Year Ended December 31, 20--

Capital Stock:				
Per Share				
January 1, 20--, Shares Issued				
Issued during Current Year,				
Balance, December 31, 20--, Shares Issued				
Retained Earnings:				
Balance, January 1, 20--				
Net Income after Federal Income Tax for 20--				
Less Dividends Declared during 20--				
Net Increase during 20--				
Balance, December 31, 20--				
Total Stockholders' Equity, December 31, 20--				

4-8 MASTERY PROBLEM (continued)

[5]

Home Plate Sporting Goods
Balance Sheet
December 31, 20--

Assets					
Current Assets:					
Cash					
Petty Cash					
Accounts Receivable					
Less Allowance for Uncollectible Accounts					
Merchandise Inventory—Softball					
Merchandise Inventory—Baseball					
Supplies—Office					
Supplies—Store					
Prepaid Insurance					
Total Current Assets					
Plant Assets:					
Office Equipment					
Less Accumulated Depr.—Office Equipment					
Store Equipment					
Less Accumulated Depr.—Store Equipment					
Total Plant Assets					
Total Assets					
Liabilities					
Current Liabilities:					
Accounts Payable					
Employee Income Tax Payable—Federal					
Employee Income Tax Payable—State					
Federal Income Tax Payable					
Social Security Tax Payable					
Medicare Tax Payable					
Sales Tax Payable					
Unemployment Tax Payable—Federal					
Unemployment Tax Payable—State					
Health Insurance Premiums Payable					
Total Liabilities					

4-8 MASTERY PROBLEM (continued)

[5]

Home Plate Sporting Goods
Balance Sheet (continued)
December 31, 20--

Stockholders' Equity						
Capital Stock						
Retained Earnings						
Total Stockholders' Equity						
Total Liabilities & Stockholders' Equity						

4-8 MASTERY PROBLEM (continued)

[6, 7]

GENERAL JOURNAL
PAGE 18

DATE	ACCOUNT TITLE	DOC. NO.	POST. REF.	DEBIT	CREDIT

4-8 MASTERY PROBLEM (concluded)

[7]

GENERAL JOURNAL   PAGE 19

	DATE	ACCOUNT TITLE	DOC. NO.	POST. REF.	DEBIT	CREDIT	
1							1
2							2
3							3
4							4
5							5
6							6
7							7
8							8
9							9
10							10
11							11
12							12
13							13
14							14
15							15
16							16
17							17
18							18
19							19
20							20
21							21
22							22
23							23
24							24
25							25
26							26
27							27
28							28
29							29
30							30
31							31

Name _____ Date _____ Class _____

4-8 MASTERY PROBLEM

Extra form

GENERAL JOURNAL PAGE ____

	DATE	ACCOUNT TITLE	DOC. NO.	POST. REF.	DEBIT	CREDIT	
1							1
2							2
3							3
4							4
5							5
6							6
7							7
8							8
9							9
10							10
11							11
12							12
13							13
14							14
15							15
16							16
17							17
18							18
19							19
20							20
21							21
22							22
23							23
24							24
25							25
26							26
27							27
28							28
29							29
30							30
31							31

Working Papers

COPYRIGHT © SOUTH-WESTERN EDUCATIONAL PUBLISHING

Name _____ Date _____ Class _____

4-9 CHALLENGE PROBLEM, p. 130

Preparing a 10-column work sheet for a departmentalized business [2]

{Note: The work sheet for this problem begins on page 146.}

4-9 CHALLENGE PROBLEM (continued)

[1]

White Cliff
Work
For Year Ended

	ACCOUNT TITLE	TRIAL BALANCE		ADJUSTMENTS	
		DEBIT	CREDIT	DEBIT	CREDIT
1	Cash	26300.71			
2	Accounts Receivable	13589.20			
3	Allowance for Uncollectible Accts.		250.00		
4	Mdse. Inventory—Skiing	111786.00			
5	Mdse. Inventory—Snowboarding	102869.11			
6	Supplies	3570.00			
7	Prepaid Insurance	1200.00			
8	Accounts Payable		57986.00		
9	Federal Income Tax Payable				
10	Capital Stock		120000.00		
11	Dividends	10000.00			
12	Retained Earnings		59723.02		
13	Income Summary—Skiing				
14	Income Summary—Snowboarding				
15	Income Summary—General				
16	Sales—Skiing		153540.00		
17	Sales—Snowboarding		118732.00		
18	Sales Ret. & Allow.—Skiing	1648.00			
19	Sales Ret. & Allow.—Snowboarding	960.00			
20	Purchases—Skiing	110030.00			
21	Purchases—Snowboarding	85670.00			
22	Purch. Ret. & Allow.—Skiing		2305.00		
23	Purch. Ret. & Allow.—Snowboarding		1786.00		
24	Salary Expense—Skiing	26759.00			
25	Salary Expense—Snowboarding	15540.00			
26	Supplies Expense				
27	Insurance Expense				
28	Uncollectible Accounts Expense				
29	Federal Income Tax Expense	4400.00			
30		514322.02	514322.02		

4-9 CHALLENGE PROBLEM (concluded)

[1]

Sport Clothing
Sheet
December 31, 20--

	ADJUSTED TRIAL BALANCE		INCOME STATEMENT		BALANCE SHEET	
	DEBIT (5)	CREDIT (6)	DEBIT (7)	CREDIT (8)	DEBIT (9)	CREDIT (10)
1						
2						
3						
4						
5						
6						
7						
8						
9						
10						
11						
12						
13						
14						
15						
16						
17						
18						
19						
20						
21						
22						
23						
24						
25						
26						
27						
28						
29						
30						
31						
32						

4-9 CHALLENGE PROBLEM

Extra form

Name _____ Date _____ Class _____

1 REINFORCEMENT ACTIVITY, page 135

[1]

ESTIMATED MERCHANDISE INVENTORY SHEET
Gross Profit Method

DEPARTMENT _____   DATE _____

1	Beginning inventory, January 1	$ _____
2	Net purchases to date	_____
3	Merchandise available for sale	$ _____
4	Net sales to date .... $ _____	
5	Less estimated gross profit .... _____	
	(Net sales × Estimated gross profit _____%)	
6	Estimated cost of merchandise sold	_____
7	Estimated ending inventory	$ _____

ESTIMATED MERCHANDISE INVENTORY SHEET
Gross Profit Method

DEPARTMENT _____   DATE _____

1	Beginning inventory, January 1	$ _____
2	Net purchases to date	_____
3	Merchandise available for sale	$ _____
4	Net sales to date .... $ _____	
5	Less estimated gross profit .... _____	
	(Net sales × Estimated gross profit _____%)	
6	Estimated cost of merchandise sold	_____
7	Estimated ending inventory	$ _____

1 REINFORCEMENT ACTIVITY (continued)

[2]

Campus Books, Inc.
Interim Departmental Statement of Gross Profit
For Month Ended November 30, 20--

	BOOKS	% OF NET SALES	SUPPLIES	% OF NET SALES	TOTAL	% OF NET SALES
Operating Revenue:						
Net Sales						
Cost of Merchandise Sold:						
Est. Mdse. Inv., Nov. 1						
Net Purchases						
Mdse. Available for Sale						
Less Est. End. Inv., Nov. 30						
Cost of Merchandise Sold						
Gross Profit on Operations						

Name _____ Date _____ Class _____

1 REINFORCEMENT ACTIVITY (continued)

[3, 5, 6]

SALES JOURNAL
PAGE 12

	DATE	ACCOUNT DEBITED	SALE NO.	POST. REF.	ACCOUNTS RECEIVABLE DEBIT	SALES TAX PAYABLE CREDIT	SALES CREDIT BOOKS	SALES CREDIT SUPPLIES	
1									1
2									2
3									3
4									4
5									5
6									6
7									7
8									8
9									9
10									10
11									11
12									12
13									13
14									14
15									15
16									16

SALES RETURNS AND ALLOWANCES JOURNAL
PAGE 12

	DATE	ACCOUNT CREDITED	CREDIT MEMO. NO.	POST. REF.	ACCOUNTS RECEIVABLE CREDIT	SALES TAX PAYABLE DEBIT	SALES RETURNS AND ALLOWANCES DEBIT BOOKS	SALES RETURNS AND ALLOWANCES DEBIT SUPPLIES	
1									1
2									2
3									3
4									4
5									5
6									6
7									7
8									8
9									9
10									10
11									11

1 REINFORCEMENT ACTIVITY (continued)

[3, 7]

PURCHASES JOURNAL
PAGE 12

	DATE	ACCOUNT CREDITED	PURCH. NO.	POST. REF.	ACCOUNTS PAYABLE CREDIT	PURCHASES DEBIT BOOKS	PURCHASES DEBIT SUPPLIES	
1								1
2								2
3								3
4								4
5								5
6								6
7								7
8								8
9								9

PURCHASES RETURNS AND ALLOWANCES JOURNAL
PAGE 12

	DATE	ACCOUNT DEBITED	DEBIT MEMO. NO.	POST. REF.	ACCOUNTS PAYABLE DEBIT	PURCHASES RETURNS AND ALLOWANCES CREDIT BOOKS	PURCHASES RETURNS AND ALLOWANCES CREDIT SUPPLIES	
1								1
2								2
3								3
4								4
5								5
6								6

[3]

GENERAL JOURNAL
PAGE 12

	DATE	ACCOUNT TITLE	DOC. NO.	POST. REF.	DEBIT	CREDIT	
1							1
2							2
3							3
4							4
5							5
6							6

Name _____ Date _____ Class _____

 REINFORCEMENT ACTIVITY (continued)

[3, 5, 8, 10]

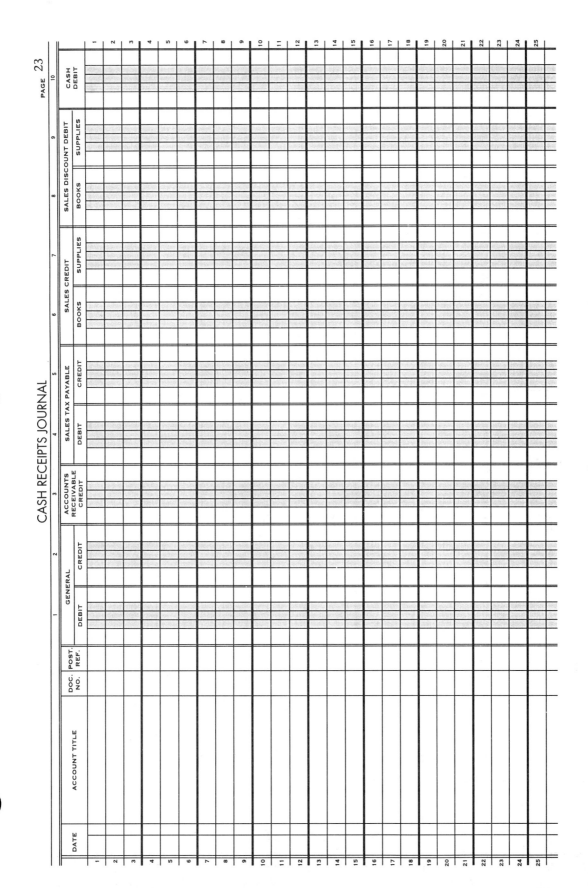

1 REINFORCEMENT ACTIVITY (continued)

[3, 5, 8, 11]

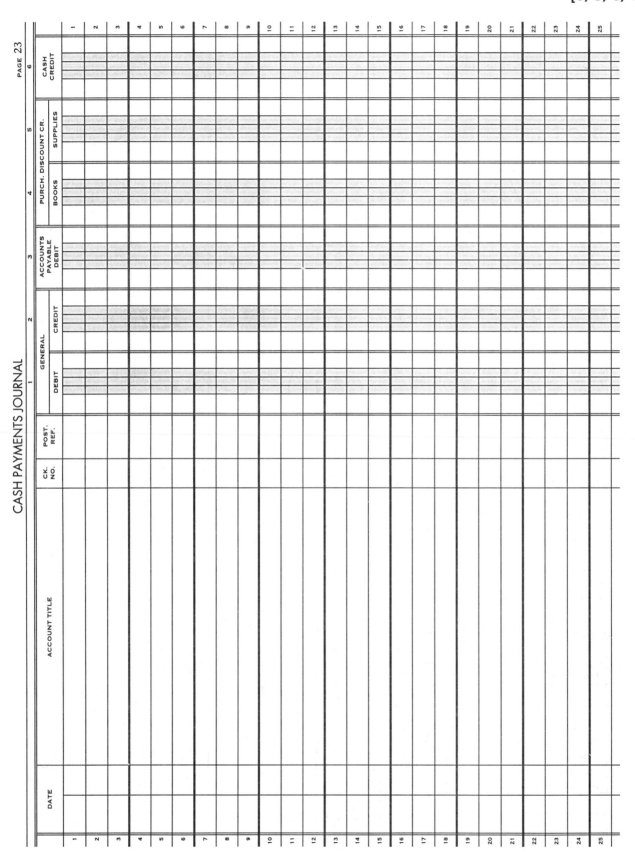

1 REINFORCEMENT ACTIVITY (continued)

[3, 5–7, 9–11, 19, 20]

GENERAL LEDGER

ACCOUNT Cash   **ACCOUNT NO.** 1105

DATE	ITEM	POST. REF.	DEBIT	CREDIT	BALANCE DEBIT	BALANCE CREDIT
20-- Dec. 1	Balance	✓			35 190 60	

ACCOUNT Petty Cash   **ACCOUNT NO.** 1110

DATE	ITEM	POST. REF.	DEBIT	CREDIT	BALANCE DEBIT	BALANCE CREDIT
20-- Dec. 1	Balance	✓			500 00	

ACCOUNT Accounts Receivable   **ACCOUNT NO.** 1115

DATE	ITEM	POST. REF.	DEBIT	CREDIT	BALANCE DEBIT	BALANCE CREDIT
20-- Dec. 1	Balance	✓			16 588 20	

ACCOUNT Allowance for Uncollectible Accounts   **ACCOUNT NO.** 1120

DATE	ITEM	POST. REF.	DEBIT	CREDIT	BALANCE DEBIT	BALANCE CREDIT
20-- Dec. 1	Balance	✓				340 20

ACCOUNT Merchandise Inventory—Books   **ACCOUNT NO.** 1125-1

DATE	ITEM	POST. REF.	DEBIT	CREDIT	BALANCE DEBIT	BALANCE CREDIT
20-- Jan. 1	Balance	✓			164 164 20	

ACCOUNT Merchandise Inventory—Supplies   **ACCOUNT NO.** 1125-2

DATE	ITEM	POST. REF.	DEBIT	CREDIT	BALANCE DEBIT	BALANCE CREDIT
20-- Jan. 1	Balance	✓			147 840 30	

ACCOUNT Supplies—Office   **ACCOUNT NO.** 1130

DATE	ITEM	POST. REF.	DEBIT	CREDIT	BALANCE DEBIT	BALANCE CREDIT
20-- Dec. 1	Balance	✓			6 080 20	

1 REINFORCEMENT ACTIVITY (continued)

[3, 5–7, 9–11, 19, 20]

GENERAL LEDGER

ACCOUNT Supplies—Store **ACCOUNT NO.** 1135

DATE	ITEM	POST. REF.	DEBIT	CREDIT	BALANCE DEBIT	BALANCE CREDIT
20-- Dec. 1	Balance	✓			4 9 6 0 80	

ACCOUNT Prepaid Insurance **ACCOUNT NO.** 1140

DATE	ITEM	POST. REF.	DEBIT	CREDIT	BALANCE DEBIT	BALANCE CREDIT
20-- Dec. 1	Balance	✓			5 2 8 0 00	

ACCOUNT Office Equipment **ACCOUNT NO.** 1205

DATE	ITEM	POST. REF.	DEBIT	CREDIT	BALANCE DEBIT	BALANCE CREDIT
20-- Dec. 1	Balance	✓			19 2 1 0 00	

ACCOUNT Accumulated Depreciation—Office Equipment **ACCOUNT NO.** 1210

DATE	ITEM	POST. REF.	DEBIT	CREDIT	BALANCE DEBIT	BALANCE CREDIT
20-- Dec. 1	Balance	✓				8 7 6 0 00

ACCOUNT Store Equipment **ACCOUNT NO.** 1215

DATE	ITEM	POST. REF.	DEBIT	CREDIT	BALANCE DEBIT	BALANCE CREDIT
20-- Dec. 1	Balance	✓			21 1 8 0 00	

ACCOUNT Accumulated Depreciation—Store Equipment **ACCOUNT NO.** 1220

DATE	ITEM	POST. REF.	DEBIT	CREDIT	BALANCE DEBIT	BALANCE CREDIT
20-- Dec. 1	Balance	✓				13 6 2 0 00

ACCOUNT Accounts Payable **ACCOUNT NO.** 2105

DATE	ITEM	POST. REF.	DEBIT	CREDIT	BALANCE DEBIT	BALANCE CREDIT
20-- Dec. 1	Balance	✓				13 1 4 5 85

REINFORCEMENT ACTIVITY (continued)

[3, 5–7, 9–11, 19, 20]

GENERAL LEDGER

ACCOUNT Employee Income Tax Payable—Federal ACCOUNT NO. 2110

DATE	ITEM	POST. REF.	DEBIT	CREDIT	BALANCE DEBIT	BALANCE CREDIT
20-- Dec. 1	Balance	✓				1 2 4 0 80

ACCOUNT Employee Income Tax Payable—State ACCOUNT NO. 2115

DATE	ITEM	POST. REF.	DEBIT	CREDIT	BALANCE DEBIT	BALANCE CREDIT
20-- Dec. 1	Balance	✓				5 6 5 40

ACCOUNT Federal Income Tax Payable ACCOUNT NO. 2120

DATE	ITEM	POST. REF.	DEBIT	CREDIT	BALANCE DEBIT	BALANCE CREDIT

ACCOUNT Social Security Tax Payable ACCOUNT NO. 2125

DATE	ITEM	POST. REF.	DEBIT	CREDIT	BALANCE DEBIT	BALANCE CREDIT
20-- Dec. 1	Balance	✓				12 8 6 1 1

ACCOUNT Medicare Tax Payable ACCOUNT NO. 2128

DATE	ITEM	POST. REF.	DEBIT	CREDIT	BALANCE DEBIT	BALANCE CREDIT
20-- Dec. 1	Balance	✓				2 9 6 79

ACCOUNT Sales Tax Payable ACCOUNT NO. 2130

DATE	ITEM	POST. REF.	DEBIT	CREDIT	BALANCE DEBIT	BALANCE CREDIT
20-- Dec. 1	Balance	✓				2 5 7 0 30

Reinforcement Activity 1 • 157

1 REINFORCEMENT ACTIVITY (continued)

[3, 5–7, 9–11, 19, 20]

GENERAL LEDGER

ACCOUNT Unemployment Tax Payable—Federal **ACCOUNT NO.** 2135

DATE	ITEM	POST. REF.	DEBIT	CREDIT	BALANCE DEBIT	BALANCE CREDIT
20-- Dec. 1	Balance	✓				3 2 80

ACCOUNT Unemployment Tax Payable—State **ACCOUNT NO.** 2140

DATE	ITEM	POST. REF.	DEBIT	CREDIT	BALANCE DEBIT	BALANCE CREDIT
20-- Dec. 1	Balance	✓				2 2 1 40

ACCOUNT Health Insurance Premiums Payable **ACCOUNT NO.** 2145

DATE	ITEM	POST. REF.	DEBIT	CREDIT	BALANCE DEBIT	BALANCE CREDIT
20-- Dec. 1	Balance	✓				1 8 8 8 00

ACCOUNT Dividends Payable **ACCOUNT NO.** 2150

DATE	ITEM	POST. REF.	DEBIT	CREDIT	BALANCE DEBIT	BALANCE CREDIT

ACCOUNT Capital Stock **ACCOUNT NO.** 3105

DATE	ITEM	POST. REF.	DEBIT	CREDIT	BALANCE DEBIT	BALANCE CREDIT
20-- Jan. 1	Balance	✓				300 0 0 0 00

ACCOUNT Retained Earnings **ACCOUNT NO.** 3110

DATE	ITEM	POST. REF.	DEBIT	CREDIT	BALANCE DEBIT	BALANCE CREDIT
20-- Jan. 1	Balance	✓				97 5 2 5 70

ACCOUNT Dividends **ACCOUNT NO.** 3115

DATE	ITEM	POST. REF.	DEBIT	CREDIT	BALANCE DEBIT	BALANCE CREDIT
20-- Dec. 1	Balance	✓			20 0 0 0 00	

REINFORCEMENT ACTIVITY (continued)

[3, 5–7, 9–11, 19, 20]

GENERAL LEDGER

ACCOUNT Income Summary—Books   ACCOUNT NO. 3120-1

DATE	ITEM	POST. REF.	DEBIT	CREDIT	BALANCE DEBIT	BALANCE CREDIT

ACCOUNT Income Summary—Supplies   ACCOUNT NO. 3120-2

DATE	ITEM	POST. REF.	DEBIT	CREDIT	BALANCE DEBIT	BALANCE CREDIT

ACCOUNT Income Summary—General   ACCOUNT NO. 3125

DATE	ITEM	POST. REF.	DEBIT	CREDIT	BALANCE DEBIT	BALANCE CREDIT

ACCOUNT Sales—Books   ACCOUNT NO. 4105-1

DATE	ITEM	POST. REF.	DEBIT	CREDIT	BALANCE DEBIT	BALANCE CREDIT
20-- Dec. 1	Balance	✓				216 920 30

ACCOUNT Sales—Supplies   ACCOUNT NO. 4105-2

DATE	ITEM	POST. REF.	DEBIT	CREDIT	BALANCE DEBIT	BALANCE CREDIT
20-- Dec. 1	Balance	✓				223 610 90

ACCOUNT Sales Discount—Books   ACCOUNT NO. 4110-1

DATE	ITEM	POST. REF.	DEBIT	CREDIT	BALANCE DEBIT	BALANCE CREDIT
20-- Dec. 1	Balance	✓			1 480 75	

1 REINFORCEMENT ACTIVITY (continued)

[3, 5–7, 9–11, 19, 20]

GENERAL LEDGER

ACCOUNT Sales Discount—Supplies   **ACCOUNT NO.** 4110-2

DATE	ITEM	POST. REF.	DEBIT	CREDIT	BALANCE DEBIT	BALANCE CREDIT
20-- Dec. 1	Balance	✓			1 8 1 0 30	

ACCOUNT Sales Returns and Allowances—Books   **ACCOUNT NO.** 4115-1

DATE	ITEM	POST. REF.	DEBIT	CREDIT	BALANCE DEBIT	BALANCE CREDIT
20-- Dec. 1	Balance	✓			1 7 6 0 00	

ACCOUNT Sales Returns and Allowances—Supplies   **ACCOUNT NO.** 4115-2

DATE	ITEM	POST. REF.	DEBIT	CREDIT	BALANCE DEBIT	BALANCE CREDIT
20-- Dec. 1	Balance	✓			2 1 3 0 20	

ACCOUNT Purchases—Books   **ACCOUNT NO.** 5105-1

DATE	ITEM	POST. REF.	DEBIT	CREDIT	BALANCE DEBIT	BALANCE CREDIT
20-- Dec. 1	Balance	✓			140 3 1 0 40	

ACCOUNT Purchases—Supplies   **ACCOUNT NO.** 5105-2

DATE	ITEM	POST. REF.	DEBIT	CREDIT	BALANCE DEBIT	BALANCE CREDIT
20-- Dec. 1	Balance	✓			137 4 9 0 20	

ACCOUNT Purchases Discount—Books   **ACCOUNT NO.** 5110-1

DATE	ITEM	POST. REF.	DEBIT	CREDIT	BALANCE DEBIT	BALANCE CREDIT
20-- Dec. 1	Balance	✓				3 1 6 0 80

REINFORCEMENT ACTIVITY (continued)

[3, 5–7, 9–11, 19, 20]

GENERAL LEDGER

ACCOUNT Purchases Discount—Supplies **ACCOUNT NO.** 5110-2

DATE	ITEM	POST. REF.	DEBIT	CREDIT	BALANCE DEBIT	BALANCE CREDIT
20-- Dec. 1	Balance	✓				3 4 2 0 30

ACCOUNT Purchases Returns and Allowances—Books **ACCOUNT NO.** 5115-1

DATE	ITEM	POST. REF.	DEBIT	CREDIT	BALANCE DEBIT	BALANCE CREDIT
20-- Dec. 1	Balance	✓				3 8 1 0 00

ACCOUNT Purchases Returns and Allowances—Supplies **ACCOUNT NO.** 5115-2

DATE	ITEM	POST. REF.	DEBIT	CREDIT	BALANCE DEBIT	BALANCE CREDIT
20-- Dec. 1	Balance	✓				4 1 2 0 70

ACCOUNT Advertising Expense **ACCOUNT NO.** 6105

DATE	ITEM	POST. REF.	DEBIT	CREDIT	BALANCE DEBIT	BALANCE CREDIT
20-- Dec. 1	Balance	✓			4 9 7 0 20	

ACCOUNT Credit Card Fee Expense **ACCOUNT NO.** 6110

DATE	ITEM	POST. REF.	DEBIT	CREDIT	BALANCE DEBIT	BALANCE CREDIT
20-- Dec. 1	Balance	✓			4 8 9 0 60	

ACCOUNT Depreciation Expense—Store Equipment **ACCOUNT NO.** 6115

DATE	ITEM	POST. REF.	DEBIT	CREDIT	BALANCE DEBIT	BALANCE CREDIT

1 REINFORCEMENT ACTIVITY (continued)

[3, 5–7, 9–11, 19, 20]

GENERAL LEDGER

ACCOUNT Salary Expense—Books　　　　　　　　　　　　　　　　ACCOUNT NO. 6120-1

DATE	ITEM	POST. REF.	DEBIT	CREDIT	BALANCE DEBIT	BALANCE CREDIT
20-- Dec. 1	Balance	✓			49 500 00	

ACCOUNT Salary Expense—Supplies　　　　　　　　　　　　　　ACCOUNT NO. 6120-2

DATE	ITEM	POST. REF.	DEBIT	CREDIT	BALANCE DEBIT	BALANCE CREDIT
20-- Dec. 1	Balance	✓			46 200 00	

ACCOUNT Supplies Expense—Store　　　　　　　　　　　　　　　ACCOUNT NO. 6125

DATE	ITEM	POST. REF.	DEBIT	CREDIT	BALANCE DEBIT	BALANCE CREDIT

ACCOUNT Depreciation Expense—Office Equipment　　　　　　ACCOUNT NO. 6205

DATE	ITEM	POST. REF.	DEBIT	CREDIT	BALANCE DEBIT	BALANCE CREDIT

ACCOUNT Insurance Expense　　　　　　　　　　　　　　　　　　ACCOUNT NO. 6210

DATE	ITEM	POST. REF.	DEBIT	CREDIT	BALANCE DEBIT	BALANCE CREDIT

ACCOUNT Miscellaneous Expense　　　　　　　　　　　　　　　ACCOUNT NO. 6215

DATE	ITEM	POST. REF.	DEBIT	CREDIT	BALANCE DEBIT	BALANCE CREDIT
20-- Dec. 1	Balance	✓			5 208 80	

1 REINFORCEMENT ACTIVITY (continued)

[3, 5–7, 9–11, 19, 20]

GENERAL LEDGER

ACCOUNT Payroll Taxes Expense **ACCOUNT NO.** 6220

DATE		ITEM	POST. REF.	DEBIT	CREDIT	BALANCE DEBIT	BALANCE CREDIT
20-- Dec.	1	Balance	✓			14 3 9 0 60	

ACCOUNT Rent Expense **ACCOUNT NO.** 6225

DATE		ITEM	POST. REF.	DEBIT	CREDIT	BALANCE DEBIT	BALANCE CREDIT
20-- Dec.	1	Balance	✓			13 2 0 0 00	

ACCOUNT Salary Expense—Administrative **ACCOUNT NO.** 6230

DATE		ITEM	POST. REF.	DEBIT	CREDIT	BALANCE DEBIT	BALANCE CREDIT
20-- Dec.	1	Balance	✓			28 6 0 0 00	

ACCOUNT Supplies Expense—Office **ACCOUNT NO.** 6235

DATE	ITEM	POST. REF.	DEBIT	CREDIT	BALANCE DEBIT	BALANCE CREDIT

ACCOUNT Uncollectible Accounts Expense **ACCOUNT NO.** 6240

DATE	ITEM	POST. REF.	DEBIT	CREDIT	BALANCE DEBIT	BALANCE CREDIT

ACCOUNT Federal Income Tax Expense **ACCOUNT NO.** 7105

DATE		ITEM	POST. REF.	DEBIT	CREDIT	BALANCE DEBIT	BALANCE CREDIT
20-- Dec.	1	Balance	✓			3 6 0 0 00	

1 REINFORCEMENT ACTIVITY (continued)

[3, 5]

ACCOUNTS RECEIVABLE LEDGER

CUSTOMER Marcello Amco   **CUSTOMER NO.** 110

DATE	ITEM	POST. REF.	DEBIT	CREDIT	DEBIT BALANCE

CUSTOMER Matthew Barasso   **CUSTOMER NO.** 120

DATE	ITEM	POST. REF.	DEBIT	CREDIT	DEBIT BALANCE

CUSTOMER Tanya Dockman   **CUSTOMER NO.** 130

DATE		ITEM	POST. REF.	DEBIT	CREDIT	DEBIT BALANCE
20-- Dec.	1	Balance	✓			504 00

CUSTOMER Brian Fadstad   **CUSTOMER NO.** 140

DATE	ITEM	POST. REF.	DEBIT	CREDIT	DEBIT BALANCE

CUSTOMER Gilmore Public Schools   **CUSTOMER NO.** 150

DATE		ITEM	POST. REF.	DEBIT	CREDIT	DEBIT BALANCE
20-- Dec.	1	Balance	✓			6240 20

CUSTOMER Belinda Judd   **CUSTOMER NO.** 160

DATE		ITEM	POST. REF.	DEBIT	CREDIT	DEBIT BALANCE
20-- Dec.	1	Balance	✓			262 50

REINFORCEMENT ACTIVITY (continued)

[3, 5]

ACCOUNTS RECEIVABLE LEDGER

CUSTOMER Janelle Kamschorr **CUSTOMER NO.** 170

DATE	ITEM	POST. REF.	DEBIT	CREDIT	DEBIT BALANCE

CUSTOMER Donald Lindgren **CUSTOMER NO.** 180

DATE	ITEM	POST. REF.	DEBIT	CREDIT	DEBIT BALANCE

CUSTOMER Renville Public Schools **CUSTOMER NO.** 190

DATE	ITEM	POST. REF.	DEBIT	CREDIT	DEBIT BALANCE
20-- Dec. 1	Balance	✓			9 5 8 1 50

[3, 5]

ACCOUNTS PAYABLE LEDGER

VENDOR A-1 Supplies **VENDOR NO.** 210

DATE	ITEM	POST. REF.	DEBIT	CREDIT	CREDIT BALANCE

VENDOR CBG Distributors **VENDOR NO.** 220

DATE	ITEM	POST. REF.	DEBIT	CREDIT	CREDIT BALANCE
20-- Dec. 1	Balance	✓			2 2 3 0 10

REINFORCEMENT ACTIVITY (continued)

[3, 5]

ACCOUNTS PAYABLE LEDGER

VENDOR Grandway Products   **VENDOR NO.** 230

DATE	ITEM	POST. REF.	DEBIT	CREDIT	CREDIT BALANCE

VENDOR H & B Books   **VENDOR NO.** 240

DATE	ITEM	POST. REF.	DEBIT	CREDIT	CREDIT BALANCE
20-- Dec. 1	Balance	✓			5430 15

VENDOR Maryland Books & Supplies   **VENDOR NO.** 250

DATE	ITEM	POST. REF.	DEBIT	CREDIT	CREDIT BALANCE
20-- Dec. 1	Balance	✓			565 40

VENDOR Oliver Books, Inc.   **VENDOR NO.** 260

DATE	ITEM	POST. REF.	DEBIT	CREDIT	CREDIT BALANCE
20-- Dec. 1	Balance	✓			4920 20

VENDOR Strup Supplies   **VENDOR NO.** 270

DATE	ITEM	POST. REF.	DEBIT	CREDIT	CREDIT BALANCE

Name _____ Date _____ Class _____

1 REINFORCEMENT ACTIVITY (continued)

[4]

RECONCILIATION OF BANK STATEMENT   Date _____

1. Enter CHECKBOOK BALANCE as shown on check stub.
2. Enter and add bank charges to obtain TOTAL BANK CHARGES.
3. Deduct TOTAL BANK CHARGES from CHECKBOOK BALANCE to obtain ADJUSTED CHECKBOOK BALANCE.
4. Enter BANK BALANCE as shown on bank statement.
5. Enter and add the amounts of any outstanding deposits recorded on the check stubs but not listed on the bank statement to obtain TOTAL OUTSTANDING DEPOSITS.
6. Add TOTAL OUTSTANDING DEPOSITS to BANK BALANCE to obtain TOTAL.
7. Sort all checks included in the statement numerically or by date issued.
    a. Check off on the check stubs of the checkbook each of the checks paid by the bank.
    b. Enter the check numbers and amounts of checks still outstanding.
    c. Add the outstanding checks to obtain TOTAL OUTSTANDING CHECKS.
8. Deduct TOTAL OUTSTANDING CHECKS from TOTAL to obtain ADJUSTED BANK BALANCE.
9. The ADJUSTED CHECKBOOK BALANCE and the ADJUSTED BANK BALANCE should agree, proving that both the checkbook balance and the bank balance are correct.

(1) CHECKBOOK BALANCE .... $ _____

BANK CHARGES

Description	Amount
Service Charge	

(2) DEDUCT TOTAL BANK CHARGES .... $ _____

(3) ADJUSTED CHECKBOOK BALANCE . $ _____

(4) BANK BALANCE .... $ _____

OUTSTANDING DEPOSITS

Date	Amount

(5) ADD TOTAL OUTSTANDING DEPOSITS .... $ _____

(6) TOTAL .... $ _____

OUTSTANDING CHECKS

CK. NO.	Amount

(7) DEDUCT TOTAL OUTSTANDING CHECKS .... $ _____

(8) ADJUSTED BANK BALANCE .... $ _____

[9]

Prove Cash:

Cash on hand at the beginning of the month .... $ _____

Plus total cash received during the month .... $ _____

Equals total .... $ _____

Less total cash paid during the month .... $ _____

Equals total cash on hand at the end of the month .... $ _____

1 REINFORCEMENT ACTIVITY (continued)

[12]

Campus Books, Inc.

Schedule of Accounts Receivable

December 31, 20--

Campus Books, Inc.

Schedule of Accounts Payable

December 31, 20--

1 **REINFORCEMENT ACTIVITY (continued)**

[15]

Campus Books, Inc.
Departmental Statement of Gross Profit
For Year Ended December 31, 20--

	BOOKS	% OF NET SALES	SUPPLIES	% OF NET SALES	TOTAL	% OF NET SALES
Operating Revenue:						
Net Sales						
Cost of Merchandise Sold:						
Mdse. Inv., Jan. 1						
Net Purchases						
Mdse. Available for Sale						
Less End. Inv., Dec. 31						
Cost of Merchandise Sold						
Gross Profit on Operations						

Reinforcement Activity 1 • **169**

1 REINFORCEMENT ACTIVITY (continued)

[13, 14]

Campus Books, Inc.
Work Sheet
For Year Ended December 31, 20--

	ACCOUNT TITLE	TRIAL BALANCE		ADJUSTMENTS		INCOME STATEMENT		BALANCE SHEET		
		DEBIT	CREDIT	DEBIT	CREDIT	DEBIT	CREDIT	DEBIT	CREDIT	
1	Cash									1
2	Petty Cash									2
3	Accounts Receivable									3
4	Allowance for Uncollectible Accounts									4
5	Mdse. Inv.—Books									5
6	Mdse. Inv.—Supplies									6
7	Supplies—Office									7
8	Supplies—Store									8
9	Prepaid Insurance									9
10	Office Equipment									10
11	Accum. Depr.—Office Equipment									11
12	Store Equipment									12
13	Accum. Depr.—Store Equipment									13
14	Accounts Payable									14
15	Employee Income Tax Pay.—Fed.									15
16	Employee Income Tax Pay.—State									16
17	Federal Income Tax Payable									17
18	Social Security Tax Payable									18
19	Medicare Tax Payable									19
20	Sales Tax Payable									20
21	Unemployment Tax Pay.—Fed.									21
22	Unemployment Tax Pay.—State									22
23	Health Ins. Prem. Payable									23
24	Dividends Payable									24
25	Capital Stock									25
26	Retained Earnings									26
27	Dividends									27
28	Income Summary—Books									28
29	Income Summary—Supplies									29
30	Income Summary—General									30

REINFORCEMENT ACTIVITY 1 (continued)

[13, 14]

	ACCOUNT TITLE	TRIAL BALANCE		ADJUSTMENTS		INCOME STATEMENT		BALANCE SHEET	
		DEBIT	CREDIT	DEBIT	CREDIT	DEBIT	CREDIT	DEBIT	CREDIT
31	Sales—Books								
32	Sales—Supplies								
33	Sales Discount—Books								
34	Sales Discount—Supplies								
35	Sales Ret. & Allow.—Books								
36	Sales Ret. & Allow.—Supplies								
37	Purchases—Books								
38	Purchases—Supplies								
39	Purchases Discount—Books								
40	Purchases Discount—Supplies								
41	Pur. Ret. & Allow.—Books								
42	Pur. Ret. & Allow.—Supplies								
43	Advertising Expense								
44	Credit Card Fee Expense								
45	Depr. Exp.—Store Equip.								
46	Salary Expense—Books								
47	Salary Expense—Supplies								
48	Supplies Expense—Store								
49	Depr. Exp.—Office Equip.								
50	Insurance Expense								
51	Miscellaneous Expense								
52	Payroll Taxes Expense								
53	Rent Expense								
54	Salary Expense—Admin.								
55	Supplies Expense—Office								
56	Uncollectible Accounts Expense								
57	Federal Income Tax Expense								
58									
59									
60									
61									

Reinforcement Activity 1 • 171

REINFORCEMENT ACTIVITY (continued)

[16]

Campus Books, Inc.
Income Statement
For Year Ended December 31, 20--

				% OF NET SALES
Operating Revenue:				
Sales:				
Less: Sales Discount				
Sales Ret. & Allow.				
Net Sales				
Cost of Merchandise Sold:				
Mdse. Inv., Jan. 1, 20--				
Purchases				
Less: Purchases Discount				
Pur. Returns & Allow.				
Net Purchases				
Total Cost of Mdse. Available				
Less Mdse. Inv., Dec. 31, 20--				
Cost of Merchandise Sold				
Gross Profit on Operations				
Operating Expenses:				
Selling Expenses:				
Advertising Expense				
Credit Card Fee Expense				
Depr. Exp.—Store Equip.				
Salary Expense—Books				
Salary Expense—Supplies				
Supplies Expense—Store				
Total Selling Expenses				
Administrative Expenses:				
Depr. Exp.—Office Equip.				
Insurance Expense				
Miscellaneous Expense				
Payroll Taxes Expense				
Rent Expense				
Salary Expense—Admin.				
Supplies Exp.—Office				

REINFORCEMENT ACTIVITY (continued)

[16]

Campus Books, Inc.
Income Statement (continued)
For Year Ended December 31, 20--

					% OF NET SALES
Uncollectible Accounts Expense					
Total Admin. Expenses					
Total Operating Expenses					
Net Income before Fed. Inc. Tax					
Less Federal Income Tax Expense					
Net Income after Fed. Inc. Tax					

[17]

Campus Books, Inc.
Statement of Stockholders' Equity
For Year Ended December 31, 20--

Capital Stock:				
Per Share				
January 1, 20--, Shares Issued				
Issued during Current Year,				
Balance, December 31, 20--, Shares Issued				
Retained Earnings:				
Balance, January 1, 20--				
Net Income after Federal Income Tax for 20--				
Less Dividends Declared during 20--				
Net Increase during 20--				
Balance, December 31, 20--				
Total Stockholders' Equity, December 31, 20--				

1 REINFORCEMENT ACTIVITY (continued)

[18]

Campus Books, Inc.
Balance Sheet
December 31, 20--

ASSETS											
Current Assets:											
Cash											
Petty Cash											
Accounts Receivable											
Less Allowance for Uncollectible Accounts											
Merchandise Inventory—Books											
Merchandise Inventory—Supplies											
Supplies—Office											
Supplies—Store											
Prepaid Insurance											
Total Current Assets											
Plant Assets:											
Office Equipment											
Less Accumulated Depr.—Office Equipment											
Store Equipment											
Less Accumulated Depr.—Store Equipment											
Total Plant Assets											
Total Assets											
LIABILITIES											
Current Liabilities:											
Accounts Payable											
Employee Income Tax Payable—Federal											
Employee Income Tax Payable—State											
Federal Income Tax Payable											
Social Security Tax Payable											
Medicare Tax Payable											
Sales Tax Payable											
Unemployment Tax Payable—Federal											
Unemployment Tax Payable—State											
Health Insurance Premiums Payable											
Total Liabilities											

REINFORCEMENT ACTIVITY (continued)

[18]

Campus Books, Inc.
Balance Sheet (continued)
December 31, 20--

STOCKHOLDERS' EQUITY			
Capital Stock			
Retained Earnings			
Total Stockholders' Equity			
Total Liabilities and Stockholders' Equity			

1 REINFORCEMENT ACTIVITY (continued)

[19, 20]

GENERAL JOURNAL — PAGE 13

	DATE	ACCOUNT TITLE	DOC. NO.	POST. REF.	DEBIT	CREDIT	
1							1
2							2
3							3
4							4
5							5
6							6
7							7
8							8
9							9
10							10
11							11
12							12
13							13
14							14
15							15
16							16
17							17
18							18
19							19
20							20
21							21
22							22
23							23
24							24
25							25
26							26
27							27
28							28
29							29
30							30
31							31

REINFORCEMENT ACTIVITY (continued)

[20]

GENERAL JOURNAL PAGE 14

	DATE	ACCOUNT TITLE	DOC. NO.	POST. REF.	DEBIT	CREDIT	
1							1
2							2
3							3
4							4
5							5
6							6
7							7
8							8
9							9
10							10
11							11
12							12
13							13
14							14
15							15
16							16
17							17
18							18
19							19
20							20
21							21
22							22
23							23
24							24
25							25
26							26
27							27
28							28
29							29
30							30
31							31

1 REINFORCEMENT ACTIVITY (concluded)

[21]

Campus Books, Inc.

Post-Closing Trial Balance

December 31, 20--

ACCOUNT TITLE	DEBIT	CREDIT

Name _____ Date _____ Class _____

5-1 WORK TOGETHER, p. 150

Preparing a voucher and journalizing vouchers in a voucher register [4]

Vchr. No. **152**

Date _____   Due Date _____   Payment Date _____

To _____

Address _____
                              Street

_____
City   State   ZIP

ACCOUNTS DEBITED	AMOUNT
PURCHASES	
SUPPLIES—SALES	
SUPPLIES—ADMIN.	
MISCELLANEOUS EXPENSE—SALES	
MISCELLANEOUS EXPENSE—ADMIN.	
RENT EXPENSE	
SALARY EXPENSE—SALES	
SALARY EXPENSE—ADMIN.	
TOTAL DEBITS	

ACCOUNTS CREDITED	AMOUNT
VOUCHERS PAYABLE	
EMPLOYEE INC. TAX PAY.—FEDERAL	
EMPLOYEE INC. TAX PAY.—STATE	
SOCIAL SECURITY TAX PAY.	
MEDICARE TAX PAY.	
TOTAL CREDITS	

Voucher Approved by _____

Recorded in Voucher
Register Page _____ by _____

Paid {
  Date _____
  Check No. _____ Amount $ _____
  Approved by _____
}

Name _____ Date _____ Class _____

5-1 WORK TOGETHER (continued)

{5, 6}

This voucher register is needed to complete Work Together 5-2.

PAGE 10

VOUCHER

	DATE	PAYEE	VCHR. NO.	PAID DATE	CK. NO.	VOUCHERS PAYABLE CREDIT	
1							1
2							2
3							3
4							4
5							5
6							6
7							7
8							8
9							9
10							10

Extra form

PAGE

VOUCHER

	DATE	PAYEE	VCHR. NO.	PAID DATE	CK. NO.	VOUCHERS PAYABLE CREDIT	
1							1
2							2
3							3
4							4
5							5
6							6
7							7
8							8
9							9
10							10

5-1 WORK TOGETHER (concluded)

[5, 6]

REGISTER
PAGE 10

	PURCHASES DEBIT (2)	SUPPLIES—SALES DEBIT (3)	SUPPLIES—ADMIN. DEBIT (4)	GENERAL ACCOUNT TITLE	POST. REF.	DEBIT (5)	CREDIT (6)	
1								1
2								2
3								3
4								4
5								5
6								6
7								7
8								8
9								9
10								10

Extra form

REGISTER
PAGE

	PURCHASES DEBIT (2)	SUPPLIES—SALES DEBIT (3)	SUPPLIES—ADMIN. DEBIT (4)	GENERAL ACCOUNT TITLE	POST. REF.	DEBIT (5)	CREDIT (6)	
1								1
2								2
3								3
4								4
5								5
6								6
7								7
8								8
9								9
10								10

Name _____ Date _____ Class _____

5-1 WORK TOGETHER

Extra form

Vchr. No.		
Date _____	Due Date _____	Payment Date _____

To _____

Address _____
                            Street

_____
City   State   ZIP

ACCOUNTS DEBITED	AMOUNT	
PURCHASES		
SUPPLIES—SALES		
SUPPLIES—ADMIN.		
MISCELLANEOUS EXPENSE—SALES		
MISCELLANEOUS EXPENSE—ADMIN.		
RENT EXPENSE		
SALARY EXPENSE—SALES		
SALARY EXPENSE—ADMIN.		
TOTAL DEBITS		

ACCOUNTS CREDITED	AMOUNT	
VOUCHERS PAYABLE		
EMPLOYEE INC. TAX PAY.—FEDERAL		
EMPLOYEE INC. TAX PAY.—STATE		
SOCIAL SECURITY TAX PAY.		
MEDICARE TAX PAY.		
TOTAL CREDITS		

Voucher Approved by _____

Recorded in Voucher
Register Page _____ by _____

Paid { Date _____
      { Check No. _____ Amount $ _____
      { Approved by _____

182 • Working Papers

5-1 ON YOUR OWN, p. 150

Preparing a voucher and journalizing vouchers in a voucher register [7]

Vchr. No. **89**		
Date _____	Due Date _____	Payment Date _____

To _____

Address _____
                    Street

_____
    City   State   ZIP

ACCOUNTS DEBITED	AMOUNT
PURCHASES	
SUPPLIES—SALES	
SUPPLIES—ADMIN.	
MISCELLANEOUS EXPENSE—SALES	
MISCELLANEOUS EXPENSE—ADMIN.	
RENT EXPENSE	
SALARY EXPENSE—SALES	
SALARY EXPENSE—ADMIN.	
TOTAL DEBITS	

ACCOUNTS CREDITED	AMOUNT
VOUCHERS PAYABLE	
EMPLOYEE INC. TAX PAY.—FEDERAL	
EMPLOYEE INC. TAX PAY.—STATE	
SOCIAL SECURITY TAX PAY.	
MEDICARE TAX PAY.	
TOTAL CREDITS	

Voucher Approved by _____

Recorded in Voucher
Register Page _____ by _____

Paid:
- Date _____
- Check No. _____ Amount $ _____
- Approved by _____

5-1 ON YOUR OWN (continued)

[8, 9]

This voucher register is needed to complete On Your Own 5-2.

PAGE 8

VOUCHER

	DATE	PAYEE	VCHR. NO.	PAID DATE	PAID CK. NO.	VOUCHERS PAYABLE CREDIT	
1							1
2							2
3							3
4							4
5							5
6							6
7							7
8							8
9							9
10							10

Extra form

PAGE

VOUCHER

	DATE	PAYEE	VCHR. NO.	PAID DATE	PAID CK. NO.	VOUCHERS PAYABLE CREDIT	
1							1
2							2
3							3
4							4
5							5
6							6
7							7
8							8
9							9
10							10

5-1 ON YOUR OWN (concluded)

[8, 9]

REGISTER PAGE 8

	PURCHASES DEBIT	SUPPLIES—SALES DEBIT	SUPPLIES—ADMIN. DEBIT	GENERAL			
	2	3	4	ACCOUNT TITLE	POST. REF.	DEBIT (5)	CREDIT (6)
1							
2							
3							
4							
5							
6							
7							
8							
9							
10							

Extra form

REGISTER PAGE

	PURCHASES DEBIT	SUPPLIES—SALES DEBIT	SUPPLIES—ADMIN. DEBIT	GENERAL			
	2	3	4	ACCOUNT TITLE	POST. REF.	DEBIT (5)	CREDIT (6)
1							
2							
3							
4							
5							
6							
7							
8							
9							
10							

Name _____ Date _____ Class _____

5-1 ON YOUR OWN

Extra form

```
Vchr.
No.
                    Due              Payment
Date _____    Date _____     Date _____
To _____
Address _____
                        Street
_____
   City              State         ZIP
```

ACCOUNTS DEBITED	AMOUNT
PURCHASES	
SUPPLIES—SALES	
SUPPLIES—ADMIN.	
MISCELLANEOUS EXPENSE—SALES	
MISCELLANEOUS EXPENSE—ADMIN.	
RENT EXPENSE	
SALARY EXPENSE—SALES	
SALARY EXPENSE—ADMIN.	
TOTAL DEBITS	

ACCOUNTS CREDITED	AMOUNT
VOUCHERS PAYABLE	
EMPLOYEE INC. TAX PAY.—FEDERAL	
EMPLOYEE INC. TAX PAY.—STATE	
SOCIAL SECURITY TAX PAY.	
MEDICARE TAX PAY.	
TOTAL CREDITS	

Voucher Approved by _____

Recorded in Voucher
Register Page _____ by _____

Paid { Date _____
      Check No. _____ Amount $ _____
      Approved by _____

186 • Working Papers   COPYRIGHT © SOUTH-WESTERN EDUCATIONAL PUBLISHING

5-2 WORK TOGETHER, p. 154

Journalizing cash payments and deposits in a check register [4-6]

The voucher register completed in Work Together 5-1 is needed to complete this Work Together.

CHECK REGISTER PAGE 10

	DATE	PAYEE	CK. NO.	VCHR. NO.	VOUCHERS PAYABLE DEBIT	PURCHASES DISCOUNT CREDIT	CASH CREDIT	BANK DEPOSITS	BANK BALANCE
1									
2									
3									
4									
5									
6									
7									
8									
9									
10									

Extra form

CHECK REGISTER PAGE

	DATE	PAYEE	CK. NO.	VCHR. NO.	VOUCHERS PAYABLE DEBIT	PURCHASES DISCOUNT CREDIT	CASH CREDIT	BANK DEPOSITS	BANK BALANCE
1									
2									
3									
4									
5									
6									
7									
8									
9									
10									

5-2 WORK TOGETHER

Extra form

CHECK REGISTER   PAGE

	DATE	PAYEE	CK. NO.	VCHR. NO.	VOUCHERS PAYABLE DEBIT	PURCHASES DISCOUNT CREDIT	CASH CREDIT	BANK DEPOSITS	BANK BALANCE
1									
2									
3									
4									
5									
6									
7									
8									
9									
10									
11									
12									
13									
14									
15									
16									
17									
18									
19									
20									
21									
22									
23									
24									
25									
26									
27									
28									
29									
30									
31									

5-2 ON YOUR OWN, p. 154

Journalizing cash payments and deposits in a check register [7–9]

The voucher register completed in On Your Own 5-1 is needed to complete this On Your Own.

CHECK REGISTER PAGE 8

	DATE	PAYEE	CK. NO.	VCHR. NO.	VOUCHERS PAYABLE DEBIT	PURCHASES DISCOUNT CREDIT	CASH CREDIT	BANK DEPOSITS	BANK BALANCE	
1										1
2										2
3										3
4										4
5										5
6										6
7										7
8										8
9										9
10										10

Extra form

CHECK REGISTER PAGE

	DATE	PAYEE	CK. NO.	VCHR. NO.	VOUCHERS PAYABLE DEBIT	PURCHASES DISCOUNT CREDIT	CASH CREDIT	BANK DEPOSITS	BANK BALANCE	
1										1
2										2
3										3
4										4
5										5
6										6
7										7
8										8
9										9
10										10

5-2 ON YOUR OWN

Extra form

CHECK REGISTER PAGE

	DATE	PAYEE	CK. NO.	VCHR. NO.	VOUCHERS PAYABLE DEBIT	PURCHASES DISCOUNT CREDIT	CASH CREDIT	BANK	
					1	2	3	DEPOSITS 4	BALANCE 5
1									
2									
3									
4									
5									
6									
7									
8									
9									
10									
11									
12									
13									
14									
15									
16									
17									
18									
19									
20									
21									
22									
23									
24									
25									
26									
27									
28									
29									
30									
31									

5-3 WORK TOGETHER

(Note: The voucher register needed for this problem begins on page 192.)

Extra forms

REGISTER — PAGE

	PURCHASES DEBIT	SUPPLIES—SALES DEBIT	SUPPLIES—ADMIN. DEBIT	GENERAL ACCOUNT TITLE	POST. REF.	DEBIT	CREDIT	
1								1
2								2
3								3
4								4
5								5
6								6
7								7
8								8
9								9
10								10

REGISTER — PAGE

	PURCHASES DEBIT	SUPPLIES—SALES DEBIT	SUPPLIES—ADMIN. DEBIT	GENERAL ACCOUNT TITLE	POST. REF.	DEBIT	CREDIT	
1								1
2								2
3								3
4								4
5								5
6								6
7								7
8								8
9								9
10								10

5-3 WORK TOGETHER, page 158

Journalizing purchases returns and allowances and payroll in a voucher register [4]

PAGE 5

VOUCHER

	DATE	PAYEE	VCHR. NO.	PAID DATE	CK. NO.	VOUCHERS PAYABLE CREDIT	
1							1
2							2
3							3
4							4
5							5
6							6
7							7
8							8
9							9
10							10

Extra form

PAGE

VOUCHER

	DATE	PAYEE	VCHR. NO.	PAID DATE	CK. NO.	VOUCHERS PAYABLE CREDIT	
1							1
2							2
3							3
4							4
5							5
6							6
7							7
8							8
9							9
10							10

5-3 WORK TOGETHER (concluded)

[4]

REGISTER
PAGE 5

	2 PURCHASES DEBIT	3 SUPPLIES—SALES DEBIT	4 SUPPLIES—ADMIN. DEBIT	GENERAL ACCOUNT TITLE	POST. REF.	5 DEBIT	6 CREDIT	
1								1
2								2
3								3
4								4
5								5
6								6
7								7
8								8
9								9
10								10

Extra form

REGISTER
PAGE

	2 PURCHASES DEBIT	3 SUPPLIES—SALES DEBIT	4 SUPPLIES—ADMIN. DEBIT	GENERAL ACCOUNT TITLE	POST. REF.	5 DEBIT	6 CREDIT	
1								1
2								2
3								3
4								4
5								5
6								6
7								7
8								8
9								9
10								10

Name _____ Date _____ Class _____

5-3 WORK TOGETHER

Extra forms

PAGE							VOUCHER 1
	DATE	PAYEE	VCHR. NO.	PAID DATE	CK. NO.	VOUCHERS PAYABLE CREDIT	
1							1
2							2
3							3
4							4
5							5
6							6
7							7
8							8
9							9
10							10

PAGE							VOUCHER 1
	DATE	PAYEE	VCHR. NO.	PAID DATE	CK. NO.	VOUCHERS PAYABLE CREDIT	
1							1
2							2
3							3
4							4
5							5
6							6
7							7
8							8
9							9
10							10

194 • Working Papers

COPYRIGHT © SOUTH-WESTERN EDUCATIONAL PUBLISHING

Name _____ Date _____ Class _____

5-3 ON YOUR OWN

(Note: The voucher register needed for this problem begins on page 196.

Extra forms

REGISTER — PAGE

	2 PURCHASES DEBIT	3 SUPPLIES—SALES DEBIT	4 SUPPLIES—ADMIN. DEBIT	GENERAL ACCOUNT TITLE	POST. REF.	5 DEBIT	6 CREDIT	
1								1
2								2
3								3
4								4
5								5
6								6
7								7
8								8
9								9
10								10

REGISTER — PAGE

	2 PURCHASES DEBIT	3 SUPPLIES—SALES DEBIT	4 SUPPLIES—ADMIN. DEBIT	GENERAL ACCOUNT TITLE	POST. REF.	5 DEBIT	6 CREDIT	
1								1
2								2
3								3
4								4
5								5
6								6
7								7
8								8
9								9
10								10

Chapter 5 A Voucher System

5-3 ON YOUR OWN, page 158

Journalizing purchases returns and allowances and payroll in a voucher register [5]

PAGE 6 — VOUCHER

	DATE	PAYEE	VCHR. NO.	PAID DATE	CK. NO.	VOUCHERS PAYABLE CREDIT	
1							1
2							2
3							3
4							4
5							5
6							6
7							7
8							8
9							9
10							10

Extra form

PAGE — VOUCHER

	DATE	PAYEE	VCHR. NO.	PAID DATE	CK. NO.	VOUCHERS PAYABLE CREDIT	
1							1
2							2
3							3
4							4
5							5
6							6
7							7
8							8
9							9
10							10

5-3 ON YOUR OWN (concluded)

[5]

REGISTER — PAGE 6

	PURCHASES DEBIT (2)	SUPPLIES—SALES DEBIT (3)	SUPPLIES—ADMIN. DEBIT (4)	GENERAL ACCOUNT TITLE	POST. REF.	DEBIT (5)	CREDIT (6)	
1								1
2								2
3								3
4								4
5								5
6								6
7								7
8								8
9								9
10								10

Extra form

REGISTER — PAGE

	PURCHASES DEBIT (2)	SUPPLIES—SALES DEBIT (3)	SUPPLIES—ADMIN. DEBIT (4)	GENERAL ACCOUNT TITLE	POST. REF.	DEBIT (5)	CREDIT (6)	
1								1
2								2
3								3
4								4
5								5
6								6
7								7
8								8
9								9
10								10

Name _____ Date _____ Class _____

5-3 ON YOUR OWN

Extra forms

PAGE   VOUCHER 1

DATE		PAYEE	VCHR. NO.	PAID DATE	CK. NO.	VOUCHERS PAYABLE CREDIT	
1							1
2							2
3							3
4							4
5							5
6							6
7							7
8							8
9							9
10							10

PAGE   VOUCHER 1

DATE		PAYEE	VCHR. NO.	PAID DATE	CK. NO.	VOUCHERS PAYABLE CREDIT	
1							1
2							2
3							3
4							4
5							5
6							6
7							7
8							8
9							9
10							10

5-1 APPLICATION PROBLEM, p. 160

Preparing a voucher and journalizing vouchers in a voucher register [1]

```
Vchr. No. 87

Date _____   Due Date _____   Payment Date _____

To _____

Address _____
                           Street

_____
         City                      State        ZIP
```

ACCOUNTS DEBITED	AMOUNT
PURCHASES	
SUPPLIES—SALES	
SUPPLIES—ADMIN.	
MISCELLANEOUS EXPENSE—SALES	
MISCELLANEOUS EXPENSE—ADMIN.	
RENT EXPENSE	
SALARY EXPENSE—SALES	
SALARY EXPENSE—ADMIN.	
TOTAL DEBITS	

ACCOUNTS CREDITED	AMOUNT
VOUCHERS PAYABLE	
EMPLOYEE INC. TAX PAY.—FEDERAL	
EMPLOYEE INC. TAX PAY.—STATE	
SOCIAL SECURITY TAX PAY.	
MEDICARE TAX PAY.	
TOTAL CREDITS	

Voucher Approved by _____

Recorded in Voucher Register Page _____ by _____

Paid { Date _____
       Check No. _____ Amount $ _____
       Approved by _____

Chapter 5   A Voucher System

5-1 APPLICATION PROBLEM (continued)

[2, 3]

The voucher register prepared in Application Problem 5-1 is needed to complete Application Problem 5-2.

PAGE 9

VOUCHER

DATE	PAYEE	VCHR. NO.	PAID DATE	CK. NO.	VOUCHERS PAYABLE CREDIT

Extra form

PAGE

VOUCHER

DATE	PAYEE	VCHR. NO.	PAID DATE	CK. NO.	VOUCHERS PAYABLE CREDIT

5-1 APPLICATION PROBLEM (concluded)

[2, 3]

The voucher register prepared in Application Problem 5-1 is needed to complete Application Problem 5-2.

REGISTER — PAGE 9

	PURCHASES DEBIT	SUPPLIES—SALES DEBIT	SUPPLIES—ADMIN. DEBIT	GENERAL ACCOUNT TITLE	POST. REF.	DEBIT	CREDIT	
1								1
2								2
3								3
4								4
5								5
6								6
7								7
8								8
9								9
10								10
11								11
12								12
13								13
14								14
15								15

Extra form

REGISTER — PAGE

	PURCHASES DEBIT	SUPPLIES—SALES DEBIT	SUPPLIES—ADMIN. DEBIT	GENERAL ACCOUNT TITLE	POST. REF.	DEBIT	CREDIT	
1								1
2								2
3								3
4								4
5								5
6								6

Name _____   Date _____   Class _____

5-1 APPLICATION PROBLEM

Extra form

Vchr. No.

Date _____   Due Date _____   Payment Date _____

To _____

Address _____
Street

_____
City   State   ZIP

ACCOUNTS DEBITED	AMOUNT
PURCHASES	
SUPPLIES—SALES	
SUPPLIES—ADMIN.	
MISCELLANEOUS EXPENSE—SALES	
MISCELLANEOUS EXPENSE—ADMIN.	
RENT EXPENSE	
SALARY EXPENSE—SALES	
SALARY EXPENSE—ADMIN.	
TOTAL DEBITS	

ACCOUNTS CREDITED	AMOUNT
VOUCHERS PAYABLE	
EMPLOYEE INC. TAX PAY.—FEDERAL	
EMPLOYEE INC. TAX PAY.—STATE	
SOCIAL SECURITY TAX PAY.	
MEDICARE TAX PAY.	
TOTAL CREDITS	

Voucher Approved by _____

Recorded in Voucher Register Page _____ by _____

Paid {
  Date _____
  Check No. _____ Amount $ _____
  Approved by _____
}

5-2 APPLICATION PROBLEM, p. 160

Journalizing cash payments and deposits in a check register [1-3]

The voucher register prepared in Application Problem 5-1 is needed to complete Application Problem 5-2.

CHECK REGISTER — PAGE 9

DATE	PAYEE	CK. NO.	VCHR. NO.	VOUCHERS PAYABLE DEBIT	PURCHASES DISCOUNT CREDIT	CASH CREDIT	BANK DEPOSITS	BANK BALANCE

5-2 APPLICATION PROBLEM

Extra form

CHECK REGISTER

DATE	PAYEE	CK. NO.	VCHR. NO.	VOUCHERS PAYABLE DEBIT	PURCHASES DISCOUNT CREDIT	CASH CREDIT	BANK DEPOSITS	BANK BALANCE

5-3 APPLICATION PROBLEM

(Note: The voucher register needed to complete this problem begins on page 206.)

Extra forms

REGISTER — PAGE ___

	PURCHASES DEBIT (2)	SUPPLIES—SALES DEBIT (3)	SUPPLIES—ADMIN. DEBIT (4)	GENERAL — ACCOUNT TITLE	POST. REF.	DEBIT (5)	CREDIT (6)
1							
2							
3							
4							
5							
6							
7							
8							
9							
10							

REGISTER — PAGE ___

	PURCHASES DEBIT (2)	SUPPLIES—SALES DEBIT (3)	SUPPLIES—ADMIN. DEBIT (4)	GENERAL — ACCOUNT TITLE	POST. REF.	DEBIT (5)	CREDIT (6)
1							
2							
3							
4							
5							
6							
7							
8							
9							
10							

Chapter 5 A Voucher System

Name _____ Date _____ Class _____

5-3 APPLICATION PROBLEM, page 161

Journalizing purchases returns and allowances in a voucher register

PAGE 2

VOUCHER

	DATE	PAYEE	VCHR. NO.	PAID		VOUCHERS PAYABLE CREDIT	
				DATE	CK. NO.		
1							1
2							2
3							3
4							4
5							5
6							6
7							7
8							8
9							9
10							10
11							11
12							12

Extra form

PAGE

VOUCHER

	DATE	PAYEE	VCHR. NO.	PAID		VOUCHERS PAYABLE CREDIT	
				DATE	CK. NO.		
1							1
2							2
3							3
4							4
5							5
6							6
7							7
8							8
9							9
10							10
11							11
12							12

5-3 APPLICATION PROBLEM (concluded)

REGISTER — PAGE 2

	PURCHASES DEBIT	SUPPLIES—SALES DEBIT	SUPPLIES—ADMIN. DEBIT	GENERAL ACCOUNT TITLE	POST. REF.	DEBIT	CREDIT	
1								1
2								2
3								3
4								4
5								5
6								6
7								7
8								8
9								9
10								10
11								11
12								12

Extra form

REGISTER — PAGE

	PURCHASES DEBIT	SUPPLIES—SALES DEBIT	SUPPLIES—ADMIN. DEBIT	GENERAL ACCOUNT TITLE	POST. REF.	DEBIT	CREDIT	
1								1
2								2
3								3
4								4
5								5
6								6
7								7
8								8
9								9
10								10
11								11
12								12

5-3 APPLICATION PROBLEM

Extra forms

PAGE   VOUCHER 1

	DATE	PAYEE	VCHR. NO.	PAID DATE	CK. NO.	VOUCHERS PAYABLE CREDIT	
1							1
2							2
3							3
4							4
5							5
6							6
7							7
8							8
9							9
10							10

PAGE   VOUCHER 1

	DATE	PAYEE	VCHR. NO.	PAID DATE	CK. NO.	VOUCHERS PAYABLE CREDIT	
1							1
2							2
3							3
4							4
5							5
6							6
7							7
8							8
9							9
10							10

Name _____ Date _____ Class _____

5-4 APPLICATION PROBLEM, p. 161

Preparing and journalizing a voucher for payroll [1, 2]

(Note: The inside of the voucher appears on page 212.)

Vchr. No. **51**

Date _____ Due Date _____ Payment Date _____

To _____

Address _____
Street

_____
City   State   ZIP

ACCOUNTS DEBITED	AMOUNT
PURCHASES	
SUPPLIES—SALES	
SUPPLIES—ADMIN.	
MISCELLANEOUS EXPENSE—SALES	
MISCELLANEOUS EXPENSE—ADMIN.	
RENT EXPENSE	
SALARY EXPENSE—SALES	
SALARY EXPENSE—ADMIN.	
TOTAL DEBITS	

ACCOUNTS CREDITED	AMOUNT
VOUCHERS PAYABLE	
EMPLOYEE INC. TAX PAY.—FEDERAL	
EMPLOYEE INC. TAX PAY.—STATE	
SOCIAL SECURITY TAX PAY.	
MEDICARE TAX PAY.	
TOTAL CREDITS	

Voucher Approved by _____

Recorded in Voucher
Register Page _____ by _____

Paid { Date _____
Check No. _____ Amount $ _____
Approved by _____

Chapter 5 A Voucher System • **209**

5-4 APPLICATION PROBLEM (continued)

[2]

PAGE 5

VOUCHER

	DATE	PAYEE	VCHR. NO.	PAID DATE	CK. NO.	VOUCHERS PAYABLE CREDIT	
1							1
2							2
3							3
4							4
5							5
6							6
7							7
8							8
9							9
10							10

Extra form

PAGE

VOUCHER

	DATE	PAYEE	VCHR. NO.	PAID DATE	CK. NO.	VOUCHERS PAYABLE CREDIT	
1							1
2							2
3							3
4							4
5							5
6							6
7							7
8							8
9							9
10							10

5-4 APPLICATION PROBLEM (continued)

[2]

REGISTER
PAGE 5

	2	3	4	\<GENERAL\>				
	PURCHASES DEBIT	SUPPLIES—SALES DEBIT	SUPPLIES—ADMIN. DEBIT	ACCOUNT TITLE	POST. REF.	DEBIT	CREDIT	
1								1
2								2
3								3
4								4
5								5
6								6
7								7
8								8
9								9
10								10

Extra form

REGISTER
PAGE

	2	3	4	\<GENERAL\>				
	PURCHASES DEBIT	SUPPLIES—SALES DEBIT	SUPPLIES—ADMIN. DEBIT	ACCOUNT TITLE	POST. REF.	DEBIT	CREDIT	
1								1
2								2
3								3
4								4
5								5
6								6
7								7
8								8
9								9
10								10

Name _____ Date _____ Class _____

5-4 APPLICATION PROBLEM (concluded)

[1, 2]

	VOUCHER	Vchr. No. **51**
	Payment Date _____ 20___	
Date _____ 20___ Terms _____	Due _____ 20___	
To _____		
Address _____		
City _____ State _____ ZIP _____		

For the following: Enclose all invoices or other papers.

DATE	VOUCHER DETAILS	AMOUNT

5-5 MASTERY PROBLEM, p. 162

Journalizing transactions in a voucher system [1–3]

CHECK REGISTER PAGE 20

	DATE	PAYEE	CK. NO.	VCHR. NO.	VOUCHERS PAYABLE DEBIT	PURCHASES DISCOUNT CREDIT	CASH CREDIT	BANK DEPOSITS	BANK BALANCE	
1										1
2										2
3										3
4										4
5										5
6										6
7										7
8										8
9										9
10										10
11										11
12										12
13										13
14										14
15										15
16										16
17										17
18										18
19										19
20										20
21										21
22										22
23										23
24										24
25										25
26										26
27										27
28										28
29										29
30										30
31										31

5-5 MASTERY PROBLEM (continued)

[2, 3]

PAGE 22

VOUCHER

	DATE	PAYEE	VCHR. NO.	PAID DATE	CK. NO.	VOUCHERS PAYABLE CREDIT	
1							1
2							2
3							3
4							4
5							5
6							6
7							7
8							8
9							9
10							10
11							11
12							12
13							13
14							14
15							15
16							16
17							17
18							18
19							19
20							20
21							21
22							22
23							23
24							24
25							25
26							26
27							27
28							28
29							29
30							30
31							31

5-5 MASTERY PROBLEM (concluded)

[2, 3]

REGISTER PAGE 22

	PURCHASES DEBIT (2)	SUPPLIES—SALES DEBIT (3)	SUPPLIES—ADMIN. DEBIT (4)	GENERAL — ACCOUNT TITLE	POST. REF.	DEBIT (5)	CREDIT (6)	
1								1
2								2
3								3
4								4
5								5
6								6
7								7
8								8
9								9
10								10
11								11
12								12
13								13
14								14
15								15
16								16
17								17
18								18
19								19
20								20
21								21
22								22
23								23
24								24
25								25
26								26
27								27
28								28
29								29
30								30
31								31

5-5 MASTERY PROBLEM

Extra form

CHECK REGISTER

	DATE	PAYEE	CK. NO.	VCHR. NO.	VOUCHERS PAYABLE DEBIT	PURCHASES DISCOUNT CREDIT	CASH CREDIT	BANK DEPOSITS	BANK BALANCE	
1										1
2										2
3										3
4										4
5										5
6										6
7										7
8										8
9										9
10										10
11										11
12										12
13										13
14										14
15										15
16										16
17										17
18										18
19										19
20										20
21										21
22										22
23										23
24										24
25										25
26										26
27										27
28										28
29										29
30										30
31										31

5-6 CHALLENGE PROBLEM, p. 162

Journalizing purchases invoices at the net amount in a voucher system [1–3]

CHECK REGISTER — PAGE 20

DATE	PAYEE	CK. NO.	VCHR. NO.	VOUCHERS PAYABLE DEBIT	CASH CREDIT	BANK DEPOSITS	BANK BALANCE

5-6 CHALLENGE PROBLEM (continued)

[2, 3]

PAGE 25

VOUCHER

	DATE	PAYEE	VCHR. NO.	PAID DATE	CK. NO.	VOUCHERS PAYABLE CREDIT	
1							1
2							2
3							3
4							4
5							5
6							6
7							7
8							8
9							9
10							10
11							11
12							12
13							13
14							14
15							15
16							16
17							17
18							18
19							19
20							20
21							21
22							22
23							23
24							24
25							25
26							26
27							27
28							28
29							29
30							30
31							31

5-6 CHALLENGE PROBLEM (concluded)

[2, 3]

REGISTER — PAGE 25

	PURCHASES DEBIT (2)	DISCOUNTS LOST DEBIT (3)	SUPPLIES DEBIT (4)	GENERAL ACCOUNT TITLE	POST. REF.	GENERAL DEBIT (5)	GENERAL CREDIT (6)	
1								1
2								2
3								3
4								4
5								5
6								6
7								7
8								8
9								9
10								10
11								11
12								12
13								13
14								14
15								15
16								16
17								17
18								18
19								19
20								20
21								21
22								22
23								23
24								24
25								25
26								26
27								27
28								28
29								29
30								30
31								31

5-6 CHALLENGE PROBLEM

Extra form

CHECK REGISTER

	DATE	PAYEE	CK. NO.	VCHR. NO.	VOUCHERS PAYABLE DEBIT	PURCHASES DISCOUNT CREDIT	CASH CREDIT	BANK DEPOSITS	BANK BALANCE	
1										1
2										2
3										3
4										4
5										5
6										6
7										7
8										8
9										9
10										10
11										11
12										12
13										13
14										14
15										15
16										16
17										17
18										18
19										19
20										20
21										21
22										22
23										23
24										24
25										25
26										26
27										27
28										28
29										29
30										30
31										31

Name _____ Date _____ Class _____

6-1 WORK TOGETHER ON YOUR OWN, p. 172

Completing a stock record for a perpetual inventory system and comparing it to an inventory record [4–7]

INVENTORY RECORD

DATE 9/30/--   ITEM Televisions

1	2	3	4	5
STOCK NUMBER	DESCRIPTION	NO. OF UNITS ON HAND	UNIT PRICE	TOTAL COST
K087	19" color television	85	$175.00	$14,875.00

STOCK RECORD

Description _____ Stock No. _____

Reorder _____ Minimum _____ Location _____

1	2	3	4	5	6	7
INCREASES			DECREASES			BALANCE
DATE	PURCHASE INVOICE NO.	QUANTITY	DATE	SALES INVOICE NO.	QUANTITY	QUANTITY

6-1 WORK TOGETHER / ON YOUR OWN

Extra forms

STOCK RECORD

Description _____ Stock No. _____

Reorder _____ Minimum _____ Location _____

DATE	PURCHASE INVOICE NO.	QUANTITY	DATE	SALES INVOICE NO.	QUANTITY	QUANTITY
1	2	3	4	5	6	7
INCREASES			DECREASES			BALANCE

STOCK RECORD

Description _____ Stock No. _____

Reorder _____ Minimum _____ Location _____

DATE	PURCHASE INVOICE NO.	QUANTITY	DATE	SALES INVOICE NO.	QUANTITY	QUANTITY
1	2	3	4	5	6	7
INCREASES			DECREASES			BALANCE

Name _____ Date _____ Class _____

6-2 WORK TOGETHER ON YOUR OWN, p. 178

Costing ending inventory using fifo, lifo, and weighted average [5]

Fifo:

Lifo:

Weighted-average:

[6]

Fifo:

Lifo:

Weighted-average:

Chapter 6 Inventory Planning and Valuation • 223

6-2 WORK TOGETHER ON YOUR OWN (concluded)

Extra space for calculations

6-3 WORK TOGETHER, p. 183

Estimating inventory using the gross profit and retail methods [5]

ESTIMATED MERCHANDISE INVENTORY SHEET
Gross Profit Method

COMPANY _____ DATE _____

1. Beginning inventory, April 1 .... $ _____
2. Net purchases to date .... _____
3. Merchandise available for sale .... $ _____
4. Net sales to date .... $ _____
5. Less estimated gross profit .... _____
   (Net sales × Estimated gross profit ____%)
6. Estimated cost of merchandise sold .... _____
7. Estimated ending inventory .... $ _____

[6]

ESTIMATED MERCHANDISE INVENTORY SHEET
Retail Method

COMPANY _____ DATE _____

		Cost	Retail

2. Beginning inventory, April 1 .... $ _____ $ _____
3. Net purchases to date .... _____ _____
4. Merchandise available for sale .... $ _____ $ _____
5. Net sales to date .... _____
   Estimated ending inventory at retail .... $ _____
6. Estimated ending inventory at cost .... $ _____
7. (Inventory at Retail × percentage ____%)

Chapter 6 Inventory Planning and Valuation • 225

Name _____ Date _____ Class _____

6-3 WORK TOGETHER

Extra forms

ESTIMATED MERCHANDISE INVENTORY SHEET
Gross Profit Method

COMPANY _____ DATE _____

1	Beginning inventory, April 1	$ _____
2	Net purchases to date	_____
3	Merchandise available for sale	$ _____
4	Net sales to date .... $ _____	
5	Less estimated gross profit .... _____	
	(Net sales × Estimated gross profit _____%)	
6	Estimated cost of merchandise sold	_____
7	Estimated ending inventory	$ _____

ESTIMATED MERCHANDISE INVENTORY SHEET
Retail Method

COMPANY _____ DATE _____

		Cost	Retail
1			
2	Beginning inventory, April 1	$ _____	$ _____
3	Net purchases to date	_____	_____
4	Merchandise available for sale	$ _____	$ _____
5	Net sales to date		_____
	Estimated ending inventory at retail		$ _____
6	Estimated ending inventory at cost	$ _____	
7	(Inventory at Retail × percentage _____%)		

Name _____ Date _____ Class _____

6-3 ON YOUR OWN, p. 183

Estimating inventory using the gross profit and retail methods [7]

ESTIMATED MERCHANDISE INVENTORY SHEET
Gross Profit Method

COMPANY _____ DATE _____

1	Beginning inventory, October 1...		$ _____
2	Net purchases to date		_____
3	Merchandise available for sale...		$ _____
4	Net sales to date...	$ _____	
5	Less estimated gross profit	_____	
	(Net sales × Estimated gross profit _____%)		
6	Estimated cost of merchandise sold......................................		_____
7	Estimated ending inventory...		$ _____

[8]

ESTIMATED MERCHANDISE INVENTORY SHEET
Retail Method

COMPANY _____ DATE _____

		Cost	Retail
1			
2	Beginning inventory, October 1...	$ _____	$ _____
3	Net purchases to date	_____	_____
4	Merchandise available for sale...	$ _____	$ _____
5	Net sales to date...		_____
	Estimated ending inventory at retail		$ _____
6	Estimated ending inventory at cost	$ _____	
7	(Inventory at Retail × percentage _____%)		

Name _____ Date _____ Class _____

6-3 ON YOUR OWN

Extra forms

ESTIMATED MERCHANDISE INVENTORY SHEET
Gross Profit Method

COMPANY _____ DATE _____

1	Beginning inventory, October 1..	$ _____
2	Net purchases to date	_____
3	Merchandise available for sale..	$ _____
4	Net sales to date....................................... $ _____	
5	Less estimated gross profit .... _____	
	(Net sales × Estimated gross profit ____%)	
6	Estimated cost of merchandise sold...	_____
7	Estimated ending inventory...	$ _____

ESTIMATED MERCHANDISE INVENTORY SHEET
Retail Method

COMPANY _____ DATE _____

		Cost	Retail
1			
2	Beginning inventory, October 1..........................	$ _____	$ _____
3	Net purchases to date	_____	_____
4	Merchandise available for sale..........................	$ _____	$ _____
5	Net sales to date..		_____
	Estimated ending inventory at retail		$ _____
6	Estimated ending inventory at cost.....................	$ _____	
7	(Inventory at Retail × percentage ____%)		

6-1 APPLICATION PROBLEM, p. 185

Keeping perpetual inventory records [1, 2]

STOCK RECORD

Description _____ Stock No. _____

Reorder _____ Minimum _____ Location _____

DATE	PURCHASE INVOICE NO.	QUANTITY	DATE	SALES INVOICE NO.	QUANTITY	QUANTITY
1	2	3	4	5	6	7
INCREASES			DECREASES			BALANCE

STOCK RECORD

Description _____ Stock No. _____

Reorder _____ Minimum _____ Location _____

DATE	PURCHASE INVOICE NO.	QUANTITY	DATE	SALES INVOICE NO.	QUANTITY	QUANTITY
1	2	3	4	5	6	7
INCREASES			DECREASES			BALANCE

6-1 APPLICATION PROBLEM

Extra forms

STOCK RECORD

Description _____ Stock No. _____

Reorder _____ Minimum _____ Location _____

DATE	PURCHASE INVOICE NO.	QUANTITY	DATE	SALES INVOICE NO.	QUANTITY	QUANTITY
1	2	3	4	5	6	7
INCREASES			DECREASES			BALANCE

STOCK RECORD

Description _____ Stock No. _____

Reorder _____ Minimum _____ Location _____

DATE	PURCHASE INVOICE NO.	QUANTITY	DATE	SALES INVOICE NO.	QUANTITY	QUANTITY
1	2	3	4	5	6	7
INCREASES			DECREASES			BALANCE

6-2 APPLICATION PROBLEM, p. 186

Determining inventory cost using fifo, lifo, weighted average, and lower of cost or market [1–3]

Stock No.	Dec. 31 Inventory	Market Price	Inventory Costing Method									
			Fifo			Lifo			Weighted Average		
			Unit Price	Total Cost	Lower of Cost or Market	Unit Price	Total Cost	Lower of Cost or Market	Unit Price	Total Cost	Lower of Cost or Market

Highest Method: _____

Lowest Method: _____

Name _____ Date _____ Class _____

6-2 APPLICATION PROBLEM

Extra form

Stock No.	Dec. 31 Inventory	Market Price	Inventory Costing Method							
			Fifo			Lifo			Weighted Average		
			Unit Price	Total Cost	Lower of Cost or Market	Unit Price	Total Cost	Lower of Cost or Market	Unit Price	Total Cost	Lower of Cost or Market

Highest Method: _____

Lowest Method: _____

6-3 APPLICATION PROBLEM, p. 186

Estimating cost of merchandise inventory using estimating methods [1]

ESTIMATED MERCHANDISE INVENTORY SHEET
Gross Profit Method

COMPANY _____ DATE _____

1	Beginning inventory, January 1..	$_____
2	Net purchases to date...	_____
3	Merchandise available for sale..	$_____
4	Net sales to date... $_____	
5	Less estimated gross profit........................... _____	
	(Net sales × Estimated gross profit ____%)	
6	Estimated cost of merchandise sold...	_____
7	Estimated ending inventory...	$_____

Extra form

ESTIMATED MERCHANDISE INVENTORY SHEET
Gross Profit Method

COMPANY _____ DATE _____

1	Beginning inventory, January 1..	$_____
2	Net purchases to date...	_____
3	Merchandise available for sale..	$_____
4	Net sales to date... $_____	
5	Less estimated gross profit........................... _____	
	(Net sales × Estimated gross profit ____%)	
6	Estimated cost of merchandise sold...	_____
7	Estimated ending inventory...	$_____

Name _____ Date _____ Class _____

6-3 APPLICATION PROBLEM (continued)

[2]

ESTIMATED MERCHANDISE INVENTORY SHEET
Retail Method

COMPANY _____ DATE _____

		Cost	Retail
1			
2	Beginning inventory, January 1	$ _____	$ _____
3	Net purchases to date	_____	_____
4	Merchandise available for sale	$ _____	$ _____
5	Net sales to date		_____
	Estimated ending inventory at retail		$ _____
6	Estimated ending inventory at cost	$ _____	
7	(Inventory at Retail × percentage _____ %)		

Extra form

ESTIMATED MERCHANDISE INVENTORY SHEET
Retail Method

COMPANY _____ DATE _____

		Cost	Retail
1			
2	Beginning inventory, January 1	$ _____	$ _____
3	Net purchases to date	_____	_____
4	Merchandise available for sale	$ _____	$ _____
5	Net sales to date		_____
	Estimated ending inventory at retail		$ _____
6	Estimated ending inventory at cost	$ _____	
7	(Inventory at Retail × percentage _____ %)		

6-4 APPLICATION PROBLEM, p. 187

Calculating merchandise inventory turnover ratio and average number of days' sales in merchandising inventory

[1]

Corporation A:

Corporation B:

Corporation C:

[2]

Corporation A:

Corporation B:

Corporation C:

[3]

Best Turnover Ratio: _____

6-4 APPLICATION PROBLEM (concluded)

Extra space for calculations

Name _____ Date _____ Class _____

6-5 MASTERY PROBLEM, p. 187

Determining cost of merchandise inventory; estimating cost of merchandise inventory using estimating methods; calculating merchandise inventory turnover ratio and average number of days' sales in merchandise inventory

[1, 2]

Stock No.	Dec. 31 Inventory	Inventory Costing Method					
		Fifo		Lifo		Weighted Average	
		Unit Price	Total Cost	Unit Price	Total Cost	Unit Price	Total Cost
Total Cost							

[3]

Stock No.	Lifo Cost	Market Price			Lower of Cost or Market
		Inventory	Unit Price	Total Cost	

[6]

[7]

Name _____ Date _____ Class _____

6-5 MASTERY PROBLEM (concluded)

[4]

```
ESTIMATED MERCHANDISE INVENTORY SHEET
          Gross Profit Method

COMPANY _____   DATE _____

1  Beginning inventory, January 1 .................................. $_____
2  Net purchases to date ...........................................  _____
3  Merchandise available for sale .................................. $_____
4  Net sales to date ...................... $_____
5  Less estimated gross profit .............        _____
   (Net sales × Estimated gross profit ____%)
6  Estimated cost of merchandise sold ..............................  _____
7  Estimated ending inventory ...................................... $_____
```

[5]

```
ESTIMATED MERCHANDISE INVENTORY SHEET
             Retail Method

COMPANY _____   DATE _____

                                             Cost         Retail
1
2  Beginning inventory, January 1 ........ $_____   $_____
3  Net purchases to date .................  _____    _____
4  Merchandise available for sale ........ $_____   $_____
5  Net sales to date .....................               _____
   Estimated ending inventory at retail ..              $_____
6  Estimated ending inventory at cost .... $_____
7  (Inventory at Retail × percentage ____%)
```

6-6 CHALLENGE PROBLEM, p. 188

Determining the unit price of merchandise inventory purchases

[1]

[2, 3]

Stock No.	Quantity	Unit Price	Total Cost	Adjusted Unit Price	Adjusted Total Cost
A69	50	$2.00	$100.00		
V56	15	6.00	90.00		
X28	30	4.00	120.00		
W12	20	3.00	60.00		
S92	5	8.00	40.00		

Extra space for calculations

6-6 CHALLENGE PROBLEM (concluded)

Extra space for calculations

7-1 WORK TOGETHER, p. 198

Journalizing entries to write off uncollectible accounts—direct write-off method [4]

GENERAL JOURNAL PAGE 2

	DATE	ACCOUNT TITLE	DOC. NO.	POST. REF.	DEBIT	CREDIT	
1							1
2							2
3							3
4							4
5							5
6							6
7							7
8							8
9							9
10							10
11							11
12							12
13							13
14							14
15							15
16							16
17							17
18							18
19							19
20							20
21							21
22							22
23							23
24							24
25							25
26							26
27							27
28							28
29							29
30							30
31							31

7-1 WORK TOGETHER (concluded)

[4]

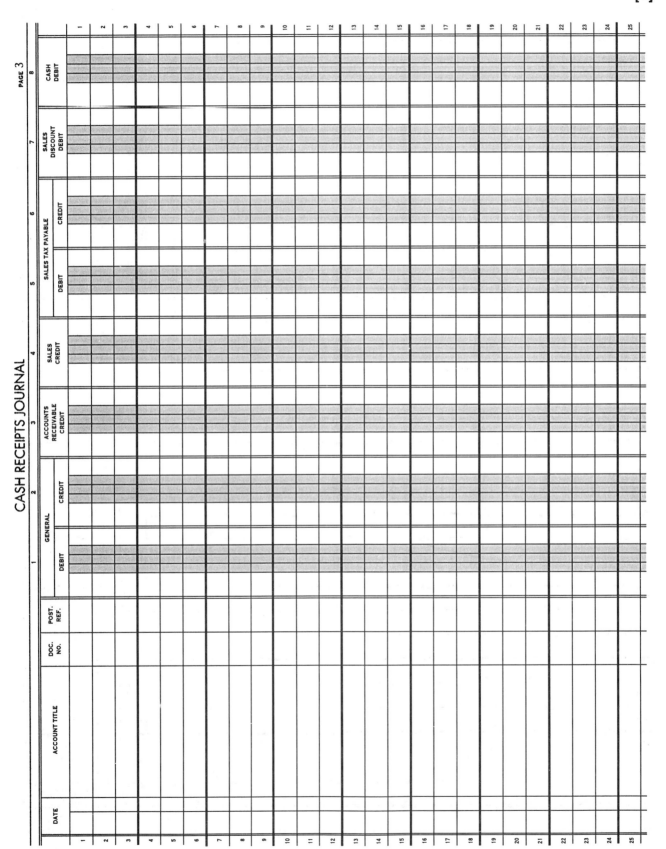

7-1 ON YOUR OWN, p. 198

Journalizing entries to write off uncollectible accounts—direct write-off method [5]

GENERAL JOURNAL
PAGE 2

	DATE	ACCOUNT TITLE	DOC. NO.	POST. REF.	DEBIT	CREDIT	
1							1
2							2
3							3
4							4
5							5
6							6
7							7
8							8
9							9
10							10
11							11
12							12
13							13
14							14
15							15
16							16
17							17
18							18
19							19
20							20
21							21
22							22
23							23
24							24
25							25
26							26
27							27
28							28
29							29
30							30
31							31

7-1 ON YOUR OWN (concluded)

[5]

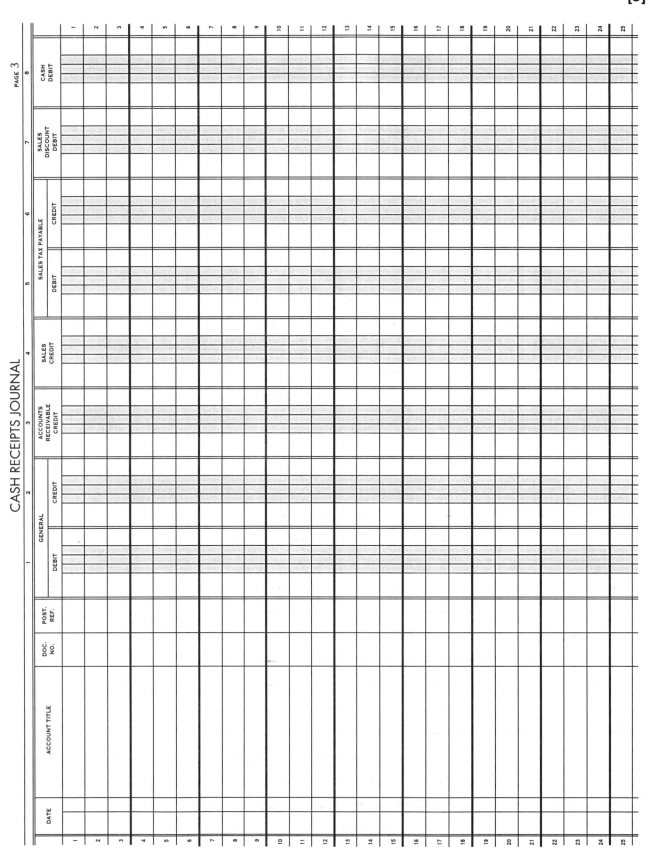

7-2 WORK TOGETHER, p. 205

Estimating amount of uncollectible accounts expense; journalizing the adjusting entry [4]

GENERAL JOURNAL PAGE 12

	DATE	ACCOUNT TITLE	DOC. NO.	POST. REF.	DEBIT	CREDIT	
1							1
2							2
3							3
4							4
5							5
6							6
7							7
8							8
9							9
10							10
11							11
12							12
13							13
14							14
15							15
16							16
17							17
18							18
19							19
20							20
21							21
22							22
23							23
24							24
25							25
26							26
27							27
28							28
29							29
30							30
31							31

7-2 WORK TOGETHER (concluded)

[5]

Age Group	Amount	Percentage	Uncollectible
Not yet due	$ 8,619.18	0.1%	
1–30 days	2,254.83	0.2%	
31–60 days	862.57	0.3%	
61–90 days	2,574.57	0.8%	
Over 90 days	350.90	50.0%	
Totals	$14,662.05		

Current Balance of Allowance for Uncollectible Accounts

Estimated Addition to Allowance for Uncollectible Accounts

GENERAL JOURNAL
PAGE 14

	DATE	ACCOUNT TITLE	DOC. NO.	POST. REF.	DEBIT	CREDIT	
1							1
2							2
3							3
4							4
5							5
6							6
7							7
8							8
9							9
10							10
11							11
12							12
13							13
14							14
15							15
16							16
17							17

7-2 ON YOUR OWN, p. 205

Estimating amount of uncollectible accounts expense; journalizing the adjusting entry [6]

GENERAL JOURNAL

PAGE 18

	DATE	ACCOUNT TITLE	DOC. NO.	POST. REF.	DEBIT	CREDIT	
1							1
2							2
3							3

7-2 ON YOUR OWN (concluded)

[7]

Age Group	Amount	Percentage	Uncollectible
Not yet due	$16,453.18	0.1%	
1–30 days	5,354.12	0.5%	
31–60 days	645.15	10.0%	
61–90 days	3,458.01	20.0%	
Over 90 days	894.28	50.0%	
Totals	$26,804.74		

Current Balance of Allowance for Uncollectible Accounts

Estimated Addition to Allowance for Uncollectible Accounts

GENERAL JOURNAL PAGE 16

DATE	ACCOUNT TITLE	DOC. NO.	POST. REF.	DEBIT	CREDIT

7-3 WORK TOGETHER, p. 208

Calculating accounts receivable turnover ratios [4]

Accounts receivable turnover ratio:

[5]

Average number of days for payment:

[6]

Is Milliken Industries effective in collecting accounts receivable?

_____
_____
_____
_____

7-3 WORK TOGETHER (concluded)

Extra space for calculations

7-3 ON YOUR OWN, p. 208

Calculating accounts receivable turnover ratios [7]

Accounts receivable turnover ratio:

[8]

Average number of days for payment:

[9]

Is Stokes Building Supply effective in collecting accounts receivable?

___
___
___
___

7-3 ON YOUR OWN (concluded)

Extra space for calculations

7-1 APPLICATION PROBLEM, p. 210

Journalizing entries to write off uncollectible accounts—direct write-off method

GENERAL JOURNAL PAGE 3

	DATE	ACCOUNT TITLE	DOC. NO.	POST. REF.	DEBIT	CREDIT	
1							1
2							2
3							3
4							4
5							5
6							6
7							7
8							8
9							9
10							10
11							11
12							12
13							13
14							14
15							15
16							16
17							17
18							18
19							19
20							20
21							21
22							22
23							23
24							24
25							25
26							26
27							27
28							28
29							29
30							30
31							31

7-1 APPLICATION PROBLEM (concluded)

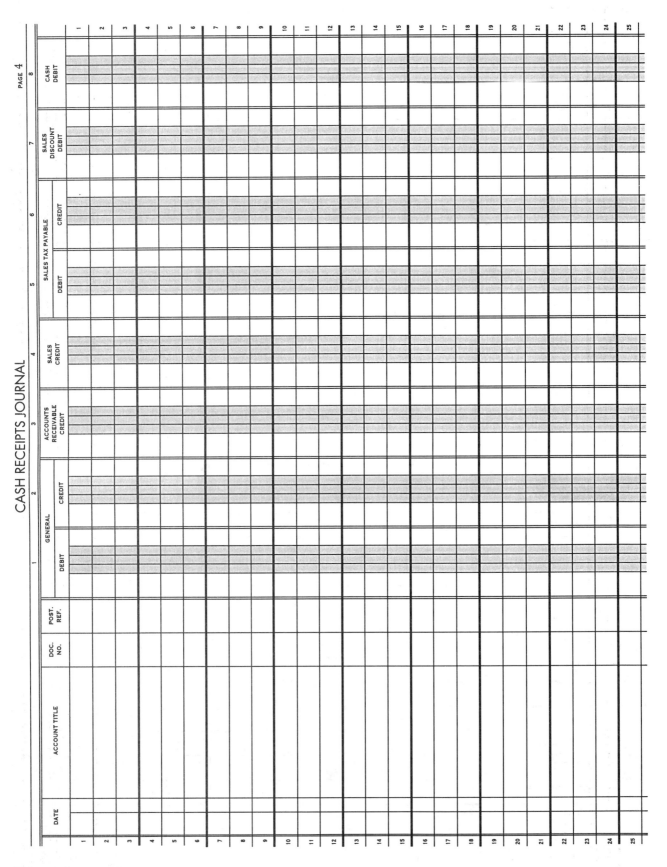

7-2 APPLICATION PROBLEM, p. 210

Estimating amount of uncollectible accounts expense by using a percentage of net sales—allowance method; journalizing the adjusting entry

GENERAL JOURNAL — PAGE 24

	DATE	ACCOUNT TITLE	DOC. NO.	POST. REF.	DEBIT	CREDIT	
1							1
2							2
3							3
4							4
5							5
6							6
7							7
8							8
9							9
10							10
11							11
12							12

Extra space for calculations

7-2 APPLICATION PROBLEM

Extra form

GENERAL JOURNAL

PAGE

DATE	ACCOUNT TITLE	DOC. NO.	POST. REF.	DEBIT	CREDIT

7-3 APPLICATION PROBLEM, p. 210

Estimating the balance of Allowance for Uncollectible Accounts by aging accounts receivable—allowance method; journalizing the adjusting entry

[1]

Age Group	Amount	Percentage	Uncollectible
Not yet due			
1–30 days			
31–60 days			
61–90 days			
Over 90 days			
Totals			
Current Balance of Allowance for Uncollectible Accounts			
Estimated Addition to Allowance for Uncollectible Accounts			

[2]

GENERAL JOURNAL PAGE 12

	DATE	ACCOUNT TITLE	DOC. NO.	POST. REF.	DEBIT	CREDIT	
1							1
2							2
3							3
4							4
5							5
6							6
7							7
8							8
9							9
10							10
11							11
12							12
13							13
14							14
15							15
16							16

7-3 APPLICATION PROBLEM

Extra form

GENERAL JOURNAL PAGE _____

DATE	ACCOUNT TITLE	DOC. NO.	POST. REF.	DEBIT	CREDIT

7-4 APPLICATION PROBLEM, p. 211

Journalizing entries to write off uncollectible accounts and collect written-off accounts—allowance method

GENERAL JOURNAL — PAGE 3

DATE	ACCOUNT TITLE	DOC. NO.	POST. REF.	DEBIT	CREDIT

7-4 APPLICATION PROBLEM (concluded)

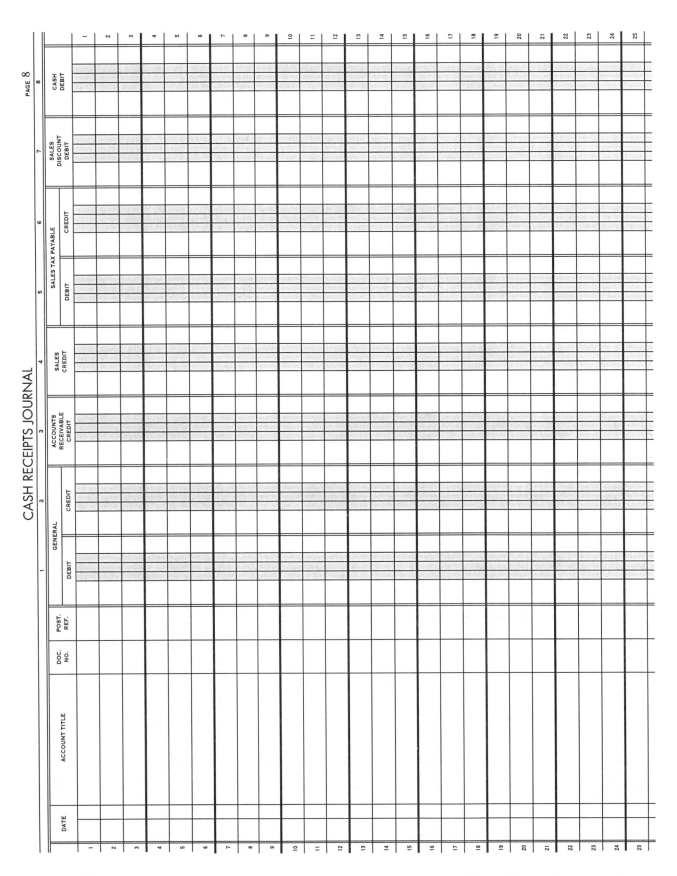

7-5 APPLICATION PROBLEM, p. 211

Calculating the accounts receivable turnover ratio

Accounts receivable turnover ratio:

[1]

[2]

Average number of days for payment:

[3]

Is Fleming Company effective in collecting its accounts receivable?

_____
_____
_____
_____

Chapter 7 Accounting for Uncollectible Accounts • 261

7-5 APPLICATION PROBLEM (concluded)

Extra space for calculations

7-6 APPLICATION PROBLEM, p. 212

Accounts receivable transactions using the allowance method

GENERAL JOURNAL

PAGE 4

DATE	ACCOUNT TITLE	DOC. NO.	POST. REF.	DEBIT	CREDIT

7-6 APPLICATION PROBLEM (concluded)

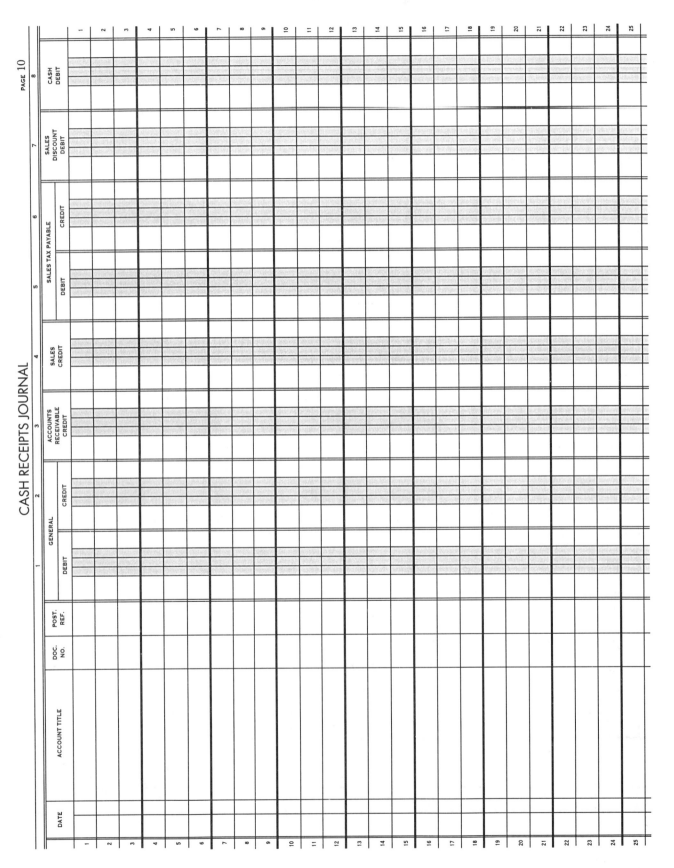

7-7 MASTERY PROBLEM, p. 212

Journalizing entries for uncollectible accounts—allowance method; calculating and journalizing the adjusting entry for uncollectible accounts expense [1, 2]

GENERAL JOURNAL PAGE 1

DATE	ACCOUNT TITLE	DOC. NO.	POST. REF.	DEBIT	CREDIT

[2]

7-7 MASTERY PROBLEM (concluded)

[1]

CASH RECEIPTS JOURNAL PAGE 1

DATE	ACCOUNT TITLE	DOC. NO.	POST. REF.	GENERAL DEBIT	GENERAL CREDIT	ACCOUNTS RECEIVABLE CREDIT	SALES CREDIT	SALES TAX PAYABLE DEBIT	SALES TAX PAYABLE CREDIT	SALES DISCOUNT DEBIT	CASH DEBIT

[3]

Average number of days for payment:

Accounts receivable turnover ratio:

7-8 CHALLENGE PROBLEM, p. 213

Estimating and journalizing uncollectible accounts expense by aging accounts receivable—allowance method; calculating and journalizing the adjusting entry for uncollectible accounts expense

[1]

Customer	Account Balance	Not Yet Due	Days Account Balance Past Due			
			1–30	31–60	61–90	Over 90
Atkins Co.	$ 2,523.64					
Bankhead Supply	2,435.75					
Coffman Distributing	943.74					
Fleet Trucking	2,643.23					
Griffin Industries	7,896.54					
Miskelly & Sons	2,754.48					
Oswalt, Inc.	8,723.54					
Rice Shipping Co.	4,363.27					
Smith Stores	1,324.76					
Totals	$33,608.95					

[2]

Age Group	Amount	Percentage	Uncollectible
Not yet due			
1–30 days			
31–60 days			
61–90 days			
Over 90 days			
Totals			

Current Balance of Allowance for Uncollectible Accounts

Estimated Addition to Allowance for Uncollectible Accounts

7-8 CHALLENGE PROBLEM (concluded)

[3]

GENERAL JOURNAL

PAGE 12

	DATE	ACCOUNT TITLE	DOC. NO.	POST. REF.	DEBIT	CREDIT	
1							1
2							2
3							3
4							4
5							5
6							6
7							7
8							8
9							9
10							10
11							11
12							12
13							13
14							14
15							15
16							16
17							17
18							18
19							19
20							20
21							21
22							22
23							23
24							24
25							25
26							26
27							27
28							28
29							29
30							30
31							31

8-1 WORK TOGETHER, p. 221

Journalizing asset purchase and property tax transactions [4]

CASH PAYMENTS JOURNAL   PAGE 1

DATE	ACCOUNT TITLE	CK. NO.	POST. REF.	GENERAL DEBIT	GENERAL CREDIT	ACCOUNTS PAYABLE DEBIT	PURCHASES DISCOUNT CREDIT	CASH CREDIT

[4]

GENERAL JOURNAL   PAGE 1

DATE	ACCOUNT TITLE	DOC. NO.	POST. REF.	DEBIT	CREDIT

8-1 WORK TOGETHER (concluded)

[5]

(Note: These records are needed to complete Work Together 8-2.)

PLANT ASSET RECORD, No. _____   General Ledger Account No. _____

Description _____   General Ledger Account _____

Date Bought _____   Serial Number _____   Original Cost _____

Estimated Useful Life _____   Estimated Salvage Value _____   Depreciation _____

Disposed of: Discarded _____   Sold _____   Traded _____

Date _____   Disposal Amount _____

YEAR	ANNUAL DEPRECIATION EXPENSE	ACCUMULATED DEPRECIATION	ENDING BOOK VALUE

[5]

PLANT ASSET RECORD, No. _____   General Ledger Account No. _____

Description _____   General Ledger Account _____

Date Bought _____   Serial Number _____   Original Cost _____

Estimated Useful Life _____   Estimated Salvage Value _____   Depreciation _____

Disposed of: Discarded _____   Sold _____   Traded _____

Date _____   Disposal Amount _____

YEAR	ANNUAL DEPRECIATION EXPENSE	ACCUMULATED DEPRECIATION	ENDING BOOK VALUE

8-1 ON YOUR OWN, p. 221

Journalizing asset purchase and property tax transactions [6]

GENERAL JOURNAL   PAGE 1

	DATE	ACCOUNT TITLE	DOC. NO.	POST. REF.	DEBIT	CREDIT	
1							1
2							2
3							3
4							4
5							5
6							6
7							7
8							8
9							9
10							10
11							11
12							12

[6]

CASH PAYMENTS JOURNAL   PAGE 1

	DATE	ACCOUNT TITLE	CK. NO.	POST. REF.	GENERAL DEBIT	GENERAL CREDIT	ACCOUNTS PAYABLE DEBIT	PURCHASES DISCOUNT CREDIT	CASH CREDIT	
1										1
2										2
3										3
4										4
5										5
6										6
7										7
8										8
9										9
10										10
11										11
12										12
13										13

Name _____ Date _____ Class _____

8-1 ON YOUR OWN (concluded)

[7]

(Note: These records are needed to complete On Your Own 8-2.)

PLANT ASSET RECORD, No. _____   General Ledger Account No. _____

Description _____   General Ledger Account _____

Date Bought _____   Serial Number _____   Original Cost _____

Estimated Useful Life _____   Estimated Salvage Value _____   Depreciation _____

Disposed of: Discarded _____   Sold _____   Traded _____

Date _____   Disposal Amount _____

YEAR	ANNUAL DEPRECIATION EXPENSE	ACCUMULATED DEPRECIATION	ENDING BOOK VALUE

[7]

PLANT ASSET RECORD, No. _____   General Ledger Account No. _____

Description _____   General Ledger Account _____

Date Bought _____   Serial Number _____   Original Cost _____

Estimated Useful Life _____   Estimated Salvage Value _____   Depreciation _____

Disposed of: Discarded _____   Sold _____   Traded _____

Date _____   Disposal Amount _____

YEAR	ANNUAL DEPRECIATION EXPENSE	ACCUMULATED DEPRECIATION	ENDING BOOK VALUE

8-2 WORK TOGETHER, p. 226

Calculating and journalizing depreciation [6]

(Note: The plant asset records from Work Together 8-1 are needed to complete this problem. The records from Work Together 8-2 are needed to complete Work Together 8-3.)

Plant asset: _____ Original cost: _____
Depreciation method: _____ Estimated salvage value: _____
　　　　　　　　　　　　　　　　　　　Estimated useful life: _____

YEAR	BEGINNING BOOK VALUE	ANNUAL DEPRECIATION	ACCUMULATED DEPRECIATION	ENDING BOOK VALUE

[6]

Plant asset: _____ Original cost: _____
Depreciation method: _____ Estimated salvage value: _____
　　　　　　　　　　　　　　　　　　　Estimated useful life: _____

YEAR	BEGINNING BOOK VALUE	ANNUAL DEPRECIATION	ACCUMULATED DEPRECIATION	ENDING BOOK VALUE

8-2 WORK TOGETHER (concluded)

GENERAL JOURNAL

PAGE 6

	DATE	ACCOUNT TITLE	DOC. NO.	POST. REF.	DEBIT	CREDIT	
1							1
2							2
3							3
4							4
5							5
6							6
7							7
8							8
9							9
10							10
11							11
12							12
13							13
14							14
15							15
16							16
17							17
18							18
19							19
20							20
21							21
22							22
23							23
24							24
25							25
26							26
27							27
28							28
29							29
30							30
31							31

Name _____ Date _____ Class _____

8-2 ON YOUR OWN, p. 226

Calculating and journalizing depreciation [9]

(Note: The plant asset records from On Your Own 8-1 are needed to complete this problem. The records from On Your Own 8-2 are needed to complete On Your Own 8-3.)

Plant asset: _____ Original cost: _____

Depreciation method: _____ Estimated salvage value: _____

Estimated useful life: _____

YEAR	BEGINNING BOOK VALUE	ANNUAL DEPRECIATION	ACCUMULATED DEPRECIATION	ENDING BOOK VALUE

[9]

Plant asset: _____ Original cost: _____

Depreciation method: _____ Estimated salvage value: _____

Estimated useful life: _____

YEAR	BEGINNING BOOK VALUE	ANNUAL DEPRECIATION	ACCUMULATED DEPRECIATION	ENDING BOOK VALUE

8-2 ON YOUR OWN (concluded)

[11]

GENERAL JOURNAL PAGE 12

	DATE	ACCOUNT TITLE	DOC. NO.	POST. REF.	DEBIT	CREDIT	
1							1
2							2
3							3
4							4
5							5
6							6
7							7
8							8
9							9
10							10
11							11
12							12
13							13
14							14
15							15
16							16
17							17
18							18
19							19
20							20
21							21
22							22
23							23
24							24
25							25
26							26
27							27
28							28
29							29
30							30
31							31

8-3 WORK TOGETHER, p. 233

Recording the disposal of plant assets [6]

(Note: The plant asset records from Work Together 8-2 are needed to complete this problem.)

PLANT ASSET RECORD, No. 127   General Ledger Account No. 1225

Description: Desk   General Ledger Account: Office Equipment

Date Bought: Apr. 4, 20X2   Serial Number: EF26796   Original Cost: $700.00

Estimated Useful Life: 5 years   Estimated Salvage Value: $200.00   Depreciation: Straight line method

Disposed of: Discarded _____   Sold _____   Traded _____

Date _____   Disposal Amount _____

YEAR	ANNUAL DEPRECIATION EXPENSE	ACCUMULATED DEPRECIATION	ENDING BOOK VALUE
20X2	$ 75.00	$ 75.00	$625.00
20X3	100.00	175.00	525.00
20X4	100.00	275.00	425.00
20X5	50.00	325.00	375.00

[6]

PLANT ASSET RECORD, No. 116   General Ledger Account No. 1245

Description: Truck   General Ledger Account: Warehouse Equipment

Date Bought: July 3, 20X1   Serial Number: 01E16742XL42   Original Cost: $38,000.00

Estimated Useful Life: 5 years   Estimated Salvage Value: $3,000.00   Depreciation: Straight line method

Disposed of: Discarded _____   Sold _____   Traded _____

Date _____   Disposal Amount _____

YEAR	ANNUAL DEPRECIATION EXPENSE	ACCUMULATED DEPRECIATION	ENDING BOOK VALUE
20X1	$3,500.00	$ 3,500.00	$34,500.00
20X2	7,000.00	10,500.00	27,500.00
20X3	7,000.00	17,500.00	20,500.00
20X4	7,000.00	24,500.00	13,500.00
20X5	7,000.00	31,500.00	6,500.00

8-3 WORK TOGETHER (continued)

[6]

PLANT ASSET RECORD, No. 106
Description: Lansing Store
Date Bought: Jan. 6, 19X7
Estimated Useful Life: 25 years
Serial Number: n/a
Estimated Salvage Value: $10,000.00
General Ledger Account No. 1215
General Ledger Account: Building
Original Cost: $60,000.00
Depreciation: Straight line method

Disposed of: Discarded ____ Sold ____ Traded ____
Date ____ Disposal Amount ____

YEAR	ANNUAL DEPRECIATION EXPENSE	ACCUMULATED DEPRECIATION	ENDING BOOK VALUE
19X7	$2,000.00	$ 2,000.00	$60,000.00
19X8	2,000.00	4,000.00	58,000.00
19X9	2,000.00	6,000.00	56,000.00
20X0	2,000.00	8,000.00	54,000.00
20X1	2,000.00	10,000.00	52,000.00
20X2	2,000.00	12,000.00	50,000.00
20X3	2,000.00	14,000.00	48,000.00
20X4	2,000.00	16,000.00	46,000.00
20X5	2,000.00	18,000.00	44,000.00

[6]

PLANT ASSET RECORD, No. 105
Description: Lansing Store
Date Bought: Jan. 6, 19X7
Estimated Useful Life: n/a
Serial Number: n/a
Estimated Salvage Value: n/a
General Ledger Account No. 1205
General Ledger Account: Land
Original Cost: $40,000.00
Depreciation: n/a

Disposed of: Discarded ____ Sold ____ Traded ____
Date ____ Disposal Amount ____

YEAR	ANNUAL DEPRECIATION EXPENSE	ACCUMULATED DEPRECIATION	ENDING BOOK VALUE

8-3 WORK TOGETHER (continued)

[5]

GENERAL JOURNAL
PAGE 1

	DATE	ACCOUNT TITLE	DOC. NO.	POST. REF.	DEBIT	CREDIT	
1							1
2							2
3							3
4							4
5							5
6							6
7							7
8							8
9							9
10							10
11							11
12							12
13							13
14							14
15							15
16							16
17							17
18							18
19							19
20							20
21							21
22							22
23							23
24							24
25							25
26							26
27							27
28							28
29							29
30							30
31							31

8-3 WORK TOGETHER (concluded)

[5]

CASH RECEIPTS JOURNAL — PAGE 3

DATE	ACCOUNT TITLE	DOC. NO.	POST. REF.	GENERAL DEBIT	GENERAL CREDIT	ACCOUNTS RECEIVABLE CREDIT	SALES CREDIT	SALES TAX PAYABLE DEBIT	SALES TAX PAYABLE CREDIT	SALES DISCOUNT DEBIT	CASH DEBIT

[5]

CASH PAYMENTS JOURNAL — PAGE 12

DATE	ACCOUNT TITLE	CK. NO.	POST. REF.	GENERAL DEBIT	GENERAL CREDIT	ACCOUNTS PAYABLE DEBIT	PURCHASES DISCOUNT CREDIT	CASH CREDIT

8-3 ON YOUR OWN, p. 233

Recording the disposal of plant assets [8]

(Note: The plant asset records from On Your Own 8-2 are needed to complete this problem.)

PLANT ASSET RECORD, No. 390   General Ledger Account No. 1205

Description: Columbus Warehouse   General Ledger Account: Land

Date Bought: Sept. 29, 20X3   Serial Number: n/a   Original Cost: $40,000.00

Estimated Useful Life: n/a   Estimated Salvage Value: n/a   Depreciation: n/a

Disposed of: Discarded _____   Sold _____   Traded _____

Date _____   Disposal Amount _____

YEAR	ANNUAL DEPRECIATION EXPENSE	ACCUMULATED DEPRECIATION	ENDING BOOK VALUE

[8]

PLANT ASSET RECORD, No. 391   General Ledger Account No. 1215

Description: Columbus Warehouse   General Ledger Account: Building

Date Bought: Sept. 29, 20X3   Serial Number: n/a   Original Cost: $50,000.00

Estimated Useful Life: 25 years   Estimated Salvage Value: $10,000.00   Depreciation: Straight line method

Disposed of: Discarded _____   Sold _____   Traded _____

Date _____   Disposal Amount _____

YEAR	ANNUAL DEPRECIATION EXPENSE	ACCUMULATED DEPRECIATION	ENDING BOOK VALUE
20X3	$ 400.00	$ 400.00	$49,600.00
20X4	1,600.00	2,000.00	48,000.00
20X5	800.00	2,800.00	47,200.00

8-3 ON YOUR OWN (continued)

[8]

PLANT ASSET RECORD, No. 369 General Ledger Account No. 1225

Description Office File Cabinet General Ledger Account Office Equipment

Date Bought July 6, 20X1 Serial Number 62B7Q76 Original Cost $500.00

Estimated Useful Life 7 years Estimated Salvage Value $80.00 Depreciation Straight line method

Disposed of: Discarded _____ Sold _____ Traded _____

Date _____ Disposal Amount _____

YEAR	ANNUAL DEPRECIATION EXPENSE	ACCUMULATED DEPRECIATION	ENDING BOOK VALUE
20X1	$30.00	$ 30.00	$470.00
20X2	60.00	90.00	410.00
20X3	60.00	150.00	350.00
20X4	60.00	210.00	290.00
20X5	45.00	255.00	245.00

[8]

PLANT ASSET RECORD, No. 428 General Ledger Account No. 1225

Description Computer General Ledger Account Office Equipment

Date Bought Jan. 3, 20X4 Serial Number 62B7QX1472 Original Cost $2,000.00

Estimated Useful Life 3 years Estimated Salvage Value $500.00 Depreciation Straight line method

Disposed of: Discarded _____ Sold _____ Traded _____

Date _____ Disposal Amount _____

YEAR	ANNUAL DEPRECIATION EXPENSE	ACCUMULATED DEPRECIATION	ENDING BOOK VALUE
20X4	$500.00	$ 500.00	$1,500.00
20X5	500.00	1,000.00	1,000.00

8-3 ON YOUR OWN (continued)

[7]

GENERAL JOURNAL
PAGE 1

DATE	ACCOUNT TITLE	DOC. NO.	POST. REF.	DEBIT	CREDIT

8-3 ON YOUR OWN (concluded)

[7]

CASH RECEIPTS JOURNAL PAGE 2

DATE	ACCOUNT TITLE	DOC. NO.	POST. REF.	GENERAL DEBIT	GENERAL CREDIT	ACCOUNTS RECEIVABLE CREDIT	SALES CREDIT	SALES TAX PAYABLE DEBIT	SALES TAX PAYABLE CREDIT	SALES DISCOUNT DEBIT	CASH DEBIT

[7]

CASH PAYMENTS JOURNAL PAGE 12

DATE	ACCOUNT TITLE	CK. NO.	POST. REF.	GENERAL DEBIT	GENERAL CREDIT	ACCOUNTS PAYABLE DEBIT	PURCHASES DISCOUNT CREDIT	CASH CREDIT

8-4 WORK TOGETHER, p. 240

Computing depreciation using various depreciation methods and calculating depletion [4]

Plant asset: _____ Original cost: _____
Depreciation method: _Double declining balance_ Estimated salvage value: _____
Estimated useful life: _____

YEAR	BEGINNING BOOK VALUE	DECLINING-BALANCE RATE	ANNUAL DEPRECIATION	ENDING BOOK VALUE

Plant asset: _____ Original cost: _____
Depreciation method: _Sum of the year's digits_ Estimated salvage value: _____
Estimated useful life: _____

YEAR	BEGINNING BOOK VALUE	FRACTION	ANNUAL DEPRECIATION	ENDING BOOK VALUE

Plant asset: _____ Original cost: _____
Depreciation method: _Production units_ Estimated salvage value: _____
Estimated useful life: _____
Depreciation rate: _____

YEAR	BEGINNING BOOK VALUE	MILES DRIVEN	ANNUAL DEPRECIATION	ENDING BOOK VALUE

8-4 WORK TOGETHER (concluded)

[4]

Plant asset: _____   Original cost: _____
Depreciation method: MACRS   Property class: _____

	YEAR	DEPRECIATION RATE	ANNUAL DEPRECIATION	

[5]

Plant asset: _____

Depletion method: Production units   Estimated total depletion: _____
Original cost: _____ Estimated useful life: _____
Estimated salvage value: _____ Depletion rate: _____

YEAR	BEGINNING BOOK VALUE	TONS RECOVERED	ANNUAL DEPRECIATION	ENDING BOOK VALUE

8-4 ON YOUR OWN, p. 241

Computing depreciation using various depreciation methods and calculating depletion [6]

Plant asset: _____ Original cost: _____
Depreciation method: _Double declining balance_ Estimated salvage value: _____
 Estimated useful life: _____

YEAR	BEGINNING BOOK VALUE	DECLINING-BALANCE RATE	ANNUAL DEPRECIATION	ENDING BOOK VALUE

Plant asset: _____ Original cost: _____
Depreciation method: _Sum of the year's digits_ Estimated salvage value: _____
 Estimated useful life: _____

YEAR	BEGINNING BOOK VALUE	FRACTION	ANNUAL DEPRECIATION	ENDING BOOK VALUE

Plant asset: _____ Original cost: _____
Depreciation method: _Production units_ Estimated salvage value: _____
 Estimated useful life: _____
 Depreciation rate: _____

YEAR	BEGINNING BOOK VALUE	PRODUCTION HOURS	ANNUAL DEPRECIATION	ENDING BOOK VALUE

8-4 ON YOUR OWN (concluded)

[6]

Plant asset: _____ Original cost: _____
Depreciation method: MACRS Property class: _____

	YEAR	DEPRECIATION RATE	ANNUAL DEPRECIATION	

[7]

Plant asset: _____

Depletion method: Production units Estimated total depletion: _____
Original cost: _____ Estimated useful life: _____
Estimated salvage value: _____ Depletion rate: _____

YEAR	BEGINNING BOOK VALUE	MCF RECOVERED	ANNUAL DEPRECIATION	ENDING BOOK VALUE

8-1 APPLICATION PROBLEM, p. 243

Journalizing entries to record buying plant assets [1]

GENERAL JOURNAL

PAGE 1

DATE	ACCOUNT TITLE	DOC. NO.	POST. REF.	DEBIT	CREDIT

[1]

CASH PAYMENTS JOURNAL

PAGE 1

DATE	ACCOUNT TITLE	CK. NO.	POST. REF.	GENERAL DEBIT	GENERAL CREDIT	ACCOUNTS PAYABLE DEBIT	PURCHASES DISCOUNT CREDIT	CASH CREDIT

Chapter 8 Accounting for Plant Assets • 289

8-1 APPLICATION PROBLEM (continued)

[2]

(Note: These plant asset records are needed to complete Application Problems 8-3. 8-4. and 8-5.)

PLANT ASSET RECORD, No. _____

General Ledger Account No. _____

Description _____   General Ledger Account _____

Date Bought _____   Serial Number _____   Original Cost _____

Estimated Useful Life _____   Estimated Salvage Value _____   Depreciation _____

Disposed of: Discarded _____   Sold _____   Traded _____

Date _____   Disposal Amount _____

YEAR	ANNUAL DEPRECIATION EXPENSE	ACCUMULATED DEPRECIATION	ENDING BOOK VALUE

PLANT ASSET RECORD, No. _____

General Ledger Account No. _____

Description _____   General Ledger Account _____

Date Bought _____   Serial Number _____   Original Cost _____

Estimated Useful Life _____   Estimated Salvage Value _____   Depreciation _____

Disposed of: Discarded _____   Sold _____   Traded _____

Date _____   Disposal Amount _____

YEAR	ANNUAL DEPRECIATION EXPENSE	ACCUMULATED DEPRECIATION	ENDING BOOK VALUE

8-1 APPLICATION PROBLEM (continued)

[2]

PLANT ASSET RECORD, No. _____   General Ledger Account No. _____

Description _____   General Ledger Account _____

Date Bought _____   Serial Number _____   Original Cost _____

Estimated Useful Life _____   Estimated Salvage Value _____   Depreciation _____

Disposed of: Discarded _____   Sold _____   Traded _____

Date _____   Disposal Amount _____

YEAR	ANNUAL DEPRECIATION EXPENSE	ACCUMULATED DEPRECIATION	ENDING BOOK VALUE

PLANT ASSET RECORD, No. _____   General Ledger Account No. _____

Description _____   General Ledger Account _____

Date Bought _____   Serial Number _____   Original Cost _____

Estimated Useful Life _____   Estimated Salvage Value _____   Depreciation _____

Disposed of: Discarded _____   Sold _____   Traded _____

Date _____   Disposal Amount _____

YEAR	ANNUAL DEPRECIATION EXPENSE	ACCUMULATED DEPRECIATION	ENDING BOOK VALUE

Name _____ Date _____ Class _____

8-1 APPLICATION PROBLEM (continued)

[2]

PLANT ASSET RECORD, No. _____   General Ledger Account No. _____

Description _____   General Ledger Account _____

Date Bought _____   Serial Number _____   Original Cost _____

Estimated Useful Life _____   Estimated Salvage Value _____   Depreciation _____

Disposed of: Discarded _____   Sold _____   Traded _____

Date _____   Disposal Amount _____

YEAR	ANNUAL DEPRECIATION EXPENSE	ACCUMULATED DEPRECIATION	ENDING BOOK VALUE

Extra form

PLANT ASSET RECORD, No. _____   General Ledger Account No. _____

Description _____   General Ledger Account _____

Date Bought _____   Serial Number _____   Original Cost _____

Estimated Useful Life _____   Estimated Salvage Value _____   Depreciation _____

Disposed of: Discarded _____   Sold _____   Traded _____

Date _____   Disposal Amount _____

YEAR	ANNUAL DEPRECIATION EXPENSE	ACCUMULATED DEPRECIATION	ENDING BOOK VALUE

8-2 APPLICATION PROBLEM, p. 243

Calculating and journalizing property tax [1]

Annual property tax calculation:

[2]

CASH PAYMENTS JOURNAL

PAGE 3

	DATE	ACCOUNT TITLE	CK. NO.	POST. REF.	GENERAL DEBIT	GENERAL CREDIT	ACCOUNTS PAYABLE DEBIT	PURCHASES DISCOUNT CREDIT	CASH CREDIT	
1										1
2										2
3										3
4										4
5										5
6										6
7										7
8										8
9										9
10										10
11										11
12										12
13										13
14										14
15										15

8-2 APPLICATION PROBLEM (concluded)

Extra form

CASH PAYMENTS JOURNAL PAGE

	DATE	ACCOUNT TITLE	CK. NO.	POST. REF.	GENERAL DEBIT	GENERAL CREDIT	ACCOUNTS PAYABLE DEBIT	PURCHASES DISCOUNT CREDIT	CASH CREDIT	
1										1
2										2
3										3
4										4
5										5
6										6
7										7
8										8
9										9
10										10
11										11
12										12
13										13
14										14
15										15
16										16
17										17
18										18
19										19
20										20
21										21
22										22
23										23
24										24
25										25
26										26
27										27
28										28
29										29
30										30
31										31
32										32

Name _____ Date _____ Class _____

8-3 APPLICATION PROBLEM, p. 243

Calculating depreciation using straight-line method

The plant asset records used in Application Problem 8-1 are needed to complete Application Problem 8-3. The depreciation tables completed in Application Problem 8-3 are needed to complete Application Problem 8-4.

Plant asset: <u>File Cabinet</u>   Original cost: _____

Depreciation method: _____   Estimated salvage value: _____

Estimated useful life: _____

YEAR	BEGINNING BOOK VALUE	ANNUAL DEPRECIATION	ACCUMULATED DEPRECIATION	ENDING BOOK VALUE

Plant asset: <u>Word Processor</u>   Original cost: _____

Depreciation method: _____   Estimated salvage value: _____

Estimated useful life: _____

YEAR	BEGINNING BOOK VALUE	ANNUAL DEPRECIATION	ACCUMULATED DEPRECIATION	ENDING BOOK VALUE

Plant asset: <u>Hand Truck</u>   Original cost: _____

Depreciation method: _____   Estimated salvage value: _____

Estimated useful life: _____

YEAR	BEGINNING BOOK VALUE	ANNUAL DEPRECIATION	ACCUMULATED DEPRECIATION	ENDING BOOK VALUE

8-3 APPLICATION PROBLEM (concluded)

Plant asset: Truck
Depreciation method: _____

Original cost: _____
Estimated salvage value: _____
Estimated useful life: _____

YEAR	BEGINNING BOOK VALUE	ANNUAL DEPRECIATION	ACCUMULATED DEPRECIATION	ENDING BOOK VALUE

Plant asset: Shelving
Depreciation method: _____

Original cost: _____
Estimated salvage value: _____
Estimated useful life: _____

YEAR	BEGINNING BOOK VALUE	ANNUAL DEPRECIATION	ACCUMULATED DEPRECIATION	ENDING BOOK VALUE

8-4 APPLICATION PROBLEM, p. 244

Journalizing annual depreciation expense [2, 4]

GENERAL JOURNAL — PAGE 12

DATE	ACCOUNT TITLE	DOC. NO.	POST. REF.	DEBIT	CREDIT

8-4 APPLICATION PROBLEM

Extra form

GENERAL JOURNAL

PAGE

DATE	ACCOUNT TITLE	DOC. NO.	POST. REF.	DEBIT	CREDIT

8-5 APPLICATION PROBLEM, p. 244

Recording disposal of plant assets [1, 3]

The plant asset records used in Application Problem 8-4 are needed to complete Application Problem 8-5.

GENERAL JOURNAL — PAGE 1

	DATE	ACCOUNT TITLE	DOC. NO.	POST. REF.	DEBIT	CREDIT	
1							1
2							2
3							3
4							4
5							5
6							6
7							7
8							8
9							9
10							10
11							11
12							12
13							13
14							14
15							15
16							16
17							17
18							18
19							19
20							20
21							21
22							22
23							23
24							24
25							25
26							26
27							27
28							28
29							29

8-5 APPLICATION PROBLEM (concluded)

[1, 3]

CASH RECEIPTS JOURNAL PAGE 6

DATE	ACCOUNT TITLE	DOC. NO.	POST. REF.	GENERAL DEBIT	GENERAL CREDIT	ACCOUNTS RECEIVABLE CREDIT	SALES CREDIT	SALES TAX PAYABLE DEBIT	SALES TAX PAYABLE CREDIT	SALES DISCOUNT DEBIT	CASH DEBIT

[1]

CASH PAYMENTS JOURNAL PAGE 12

DATE	ACCOUNT TITLE	CK. NO.	POST. REF.	GENERAL DEBIT	GENERAL CREDIT	ACCOUNTS PAYABLE DEBIT	PURCHASES DISCOUNT CREDIT	CASH CREDIT

8-6 APPLICATION PROBLEM, p. 245

Recording the sale of land and building [1]

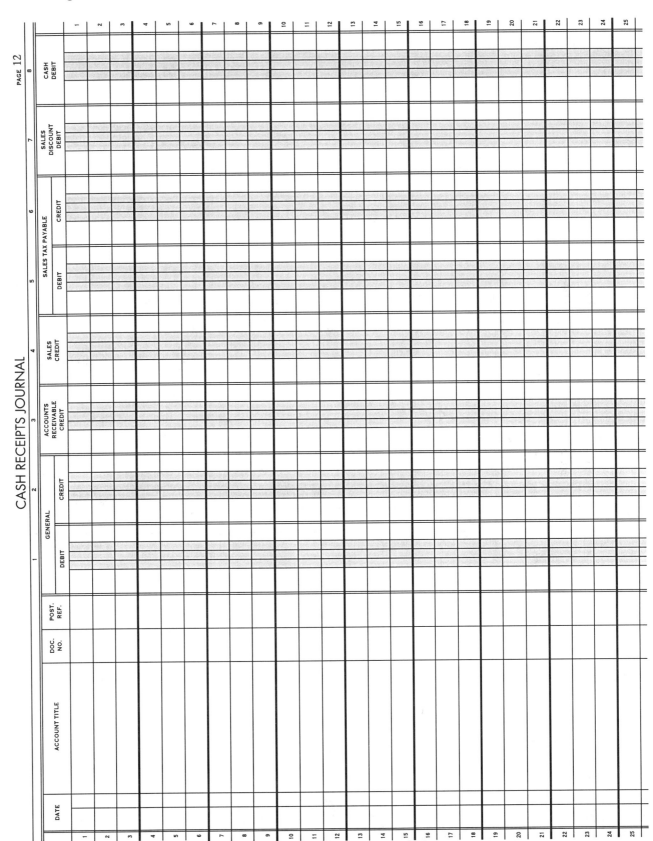

Name _____ Date _____ Class _____

8-6 APPLICATION PROBLEM (concluded)

[2]

PLANT ASSET RECORD, No. 61   General Ledger Account No. 1205
Description Jackson Warehouse   General Ledger Account Land
Date Bought Jan. 1, 20--   Serial Number n/a   Original Cost $20,000.00
Estimated Useful Life Indefinite   Estimated Salvage Value n/a   Depreciation n/a

Disposed of: Discarded _____   Sold _____   Traded _____
Date _____   Disposal Amount _____

YEAR	ANNUAL DEPRECIATION EXPENSE	ACCUMULATED DEPRECIATION	ENDING BOOK VALUE

PLANT ASSET RECORD, No. 62   General Ledger Account No. 1215
Description Jackson Warehouse   General Ledger Account Building
Date Bought Jan. 1, 20--   Serial Number None   Original Cost $100,000.00
Estimated Useful Life 25 years   Estimated Salvage Value $10,000.00   Depreciation Straight line method

Disposed of: Discarded _____   Sold _____   Traded _____
Date _____   Disposal Amount _____

YEAR	ANNUAL DEPRECIATION EXPENSE	ACCUMULATED DEPRECIATION	ENDING BOOK VALUE
20X5	$3,600.00	$61,200.00	$38,800.00

8-7 APPLICATION PROBLEM, p. 245

Calculating depreciation expense using the straight-line, declining-balance, and sum-of-the-years digits method

Plant asset: _____ Original cost: _____

Depreciation method: <u>Straight line</u> Estimated salvage value: _____

Estimated useful life: _____

YEAR	BEGINNING BOOK VALUE	ANNUAL DEPRECIATION	ACCUMULATED DEPRECIATION	ENDING BOOK VALUE

Plant asset: _____ Original cost: _____

Depreciation method: <u>Double declining balance</u> Estimated salvage value: _____

Estimated useful life: _____

YEAR	BEGINNING BOOK VALUE	DECLINING-BALANCE RATE	ANNUAL DEPRECIATION	ENDING BOOK VALUE

8-7 APPLICATION PROBLEM (concluded)

Plant asset: _____ Original cost: _____
Depreciation method: _Sum of the year's digits_ Estimated salvage value: _____
Estimated useful life: _____

YEAR	BEGINNING BOOK VALUE	FRACTION	ANNUAL DEPRECIATION	ENDING BOOK VALUE

Extra form

Plant asset: _____ Original cost: _____
Depreciation method: _____ Estimated salvage value: _____
Estimated useful life: _____

YEAR	BEGINNING BOOK VALUE	ANNUAL DEPRECIATION	ACCUMULATED DEPRECIATION	ENDING BOOK VALUE

8-8 APPLICATION PROBLEM, p. 245

Calculating depreciation expense using the production-unit method [1]

Depreciation rate calculation:

[2]

Plant asset: _____

Depreciation method: _Production units_

Original cost: _____   Estimated useful life: _____

Estimated salvage value: _____   Depreciation rate: _____ per mile driven

YEAR	BEGINNING BOOK VALUE	MILES DRIVEN	ANNUAL DEPRECIATION	ENDING BOOK VALUE
		27,500		
		26,000		
		25,000		
		21,000		
		19,000		
		118,500		

8-9 APPLICATION PROBLEM

Extra forms

Plant asset: _____ Original cost: _____

Depreciation method: _____ Estimated salvage value: _____

Estimated useful life: _____

YEAR	BEGINNING BOOK VALUE	ANNUAL DEPRECIATION	ACCUMULATED DEPRECIATION	ENDING BOOK VALUE

Plant asset: _____ Original cost: _____

Depreciation method: _____ Estimated salvage value: _____

Estimated useful life: _____

YEAR	BEGINNING BOOK VALUE	ANNUAL DEPRECIATION	ACCUMULATED DEPRECIATION	ENDING BOOK VALUE

8-9 APPLICATION PROBLEM, p. 246

Calculating depreciation expense using MACRS

Plant asset: _____ Original cost: _____

Depreciation method: MACRS Property class: _____

	YEAR	DEPRECIATION RATE	ANNUAL DEPRECIATION	
		20.00%		
		32.00%		
		19.20%		
		11.52%		
		11.52%		
		5.76%		
		100.00%		

Extra form

Plant asset: _____ Original cost: _____

Depreciation method: _____ Property class: _____

	YEAR	DEPRECIATION RATE	ANNUAL DEPRECIATION	

8-10 APPLICATION PROBLEM, p. 246

Calculating depletion expense using production-unit method

Plant asset: Mine

Depletion method: _____
Original cost: _____
Estimated salvage value: _____

Estimated total value of coal: _____
Estimated tons of recoverable coal: _____
Depletion rate: _____ per ton mined

YEAR	BEGINNING BOOK VALUE	TONS MINED	ANNUAL DEPLETION	ENDING BOOK VALUE
		9,000		
		9,400		
		7,000		
		12,500		
		8,200		
		46,100		

Extra form

Plant asset: _____

Depreciation method: _____
Original cost: _____
Estimated salvage value: _____

Estimated total value of coal: _____
Estimated tons of recoverable coal: _____
Depletion rate: _____ per ton mined

YEAR	BEGINNING BOOK VALUE	TONS MINED	ANNUAL DEPLETION	ENDING BOOK VALUE

8-11 MASTERY PROBLEM, p. 246

Recording entries for plant assets [1]

GENERAL JOURNAL — PAGE 1

DATE	ACCOUNT TITLE	DOC. NO.	POST. REF.	DEBIT	CREDIT

8-11 MASTERY PROBLEM (continued)

[1, 3]

CASH RECEIPTS JOURNAL PAGE 6

DATE	ACCOUNT TITLE	DOC. NO.	POST. REF.	GENERAL DEBIT	GENERAL CREDIT	ACCOUNTS RECEIVABLE CREDIT	SALES CREDIT	SALES TAX PAYABLE DEBIT	SALES TAX PAYABLE CREDIT	SALES DISCOUNT DEBIT	CASH DEBIT

[1]

CASH PAYMENTS JOURNAL PAGE 8

DATE	ACCOUNT TITLE	CK. NO.	POST. REF.	GENERAL DEBIT	GENERAL CREDIT	ACCOUNTS PAYABLE DEBIT	PURCHASES DISCOUNT CREDIT	CASH CREDIT

8-11 MASTERY PROBLEM (continued)

[2]

PLANT ASSET RECORD, No. 167 General Ledger Account No. 1230

Description **Desk** General Ledger Account **Office Equip.**

Date Bought **Jan. 5, 20X4** Serial Number **D3481** Original Cost **$720.00**

Estimated Useful Life **5 years** Estimated Salvage Value **$120.00** Depreciation **Straight line method**

Disposed of: Discarded _____ Sold _____ Traded _____

Date _____ Disposal Amount _____

YEAR	ANNUAL DEPRECIATION EXPENSE	ACCUMULATED DEPRECIATION	ENDING BOOK VALUE
20X4	$120.00	$120.00	$600.00
20X5	120.00	240.00	480.00
20X6	120.00	360.00	360.00
20X7	120.00	480.00	240.00
20X8	120.00	600.00	120.00

PLANT ASSET RECORD, No. 168 General Ledger Account No. 1230

Description **Table** General Ledger Account **Office Equip.**

Date Bought **Mar. 29, 20X4** Serial Number **T3929** Original Cost **$425.00**

Estimated Useful Life **5 years** Estimated Salvage Value **$25.00** Depreciation **Straight line method**

Disposed of: Discarded _____ Sold _____ Traded _____

Date _____ Disposal Amount _____

YEAR	ANNUAL DEPRECIATION EXPENSE	ACCUMULATED DEPRECIATION	ENDING BOOK VALUE
20X4	$60.00	$ 60.00	$365.00
20X5	80.00	140.00	285.00
20X6	80.00	220.00	205.00
20X7	80.00	300.00	125.00
20X8	80.00	380.00	45.00

Name _____ Date _____ Class _____

8-11 MASTERY PROBLEM (continued)

[2]

PLANT ASSET RECORD, No. 169   General Ledger Account No. 1230

Description: Filing Cabinet   General Ledger Account: Office Equip.

Date Bought: June 28, 20X0   Serial Number: FC125   Original Cost: $400.00

Estimated Useful Life: 10 years   Estimated Salvage Value: $50.00   Depreciation: Straight line method

Disposed of: Discarded _____   Sold _____   Traded _____

Date _____   Disposal Amount _____

YEAR	ANNUAL DEPRECIATION EXPENSE	ACCUMULATED DEPRECIATION	ENDING BOOK VALUE
20X0	$17.50	$ 17.50	$382.50
20X1	35.00	52.50	347.50
20X2	35.00	87.50	312.50
20X3	35.00	122.50	277.50
20X4	35.00	157.50	242.50
20X5	35.00	192.50	207.50
20X6	35.00	227.50	172.50
20X7	35.00	262.50	137.50
20X8	35.00	297.50	102.50

PLANT ASSET RECORD, No. 170   General Ledger Account No. 1230

Description: Word Processor   General Ledger Account: Office Equip.

Date Bought: Apr. 6, 20X3   Serial Number: TM48194H32   Original Cost: $750.00

Estimated Useful Life: 6 years   Estimated Salvage Value: $150.00   Depreciation: Straight line method

Disposed of: Discarded _____   Sold _____   Traded _____

Date _____   Disposal Amount _____

YEAR	ANNUAL DEPRECIATION EXPENSE	ACCUMULATED DEPRECIATION	ENDING BOOK VALUE
20X3	$ 75.00	$ 75.00	$675.00
20X4	100.00	175.00	575.00
20X5	100.00	275.00	475.00
20X6	100.00	375.00	375.00
20X7	100.00	475.00	275.00
20X8	100.00	575.00	175.00

8-11 MASTERY PROBLEM (concluded)

[2]

PLANT ASSET RECORD, No. 171 General Ledger Account No. 1230

Description: Copying Machine General Ledger Account: Office Equip.

Date Bought: July 1, 20X4 Serial Number: C56M203 Original Cost: $800.00

Estimated Useful Life: 5 years Estimated Salvage Value: $50.00 Depreciation: Straight line method

Disposed of: Discarded _____ Sold _____ Traded _____

Date _____ Disposal Amount _____

YEAR	ANNUAL DEPRECIATION EXPENSE	ACCUMULATED DEPRECIATION	ENDING BOOK VALUE
20X4	$ 75.00	$ 75.00	$725.00
20X5	150.00	225.00	575.00
20X6	150.00	375.00	425.00
20X7	150.00	525.00	275.00
20X8	150.00	675.00	125.00

PLANT ASSET RECORD, No. _____ General Ledger Account No. _____

Description _____ General Ledger Account _____

Date Bought _____ Serial Number _____ Original Cost _____

Estimated Useful Life _____ Estimated Salvage Value _____ Depreciation _____

Disposed of: Discarded _____ Sold _____ Traded _____

Date _____ Disposal Amount _____

YEAR	ANNUAL DEPRECIATION EXPENSE	ACCUMULATED DEPRECIATION	ENDING BOOK VALUE

PLANT ASSET RECORD, No. _____ General Ledger Account No. _____

Description _____ General Ledger Account _____

Date Bought _____ Serial Number _____ Original Cost _____

Estimated Useful Life _____ Estimated Salvage Value _____ Depreciation _____

Disposed of: Discarded _____ Sold _____ Traded _____

Date _____ Disposal Amount _____

8-11 MASTERY PROBLEM

Extra forms

PLANT ASSET RECORD, No. _____   General Ledger Account No. _____

Description _____   General Ledger Account _____

Date Bought _____   Serial Number _____   Original Cost _____

Estimated Useful Life _____   Estimated Salvage Value _____   Depreciation _____

Disposed of: Discarded _____   Sold _____   Traded _____

Date _____   Disposal Amount _____

YEAR	ANNUAL DEPRECIATION EXPENSE	ACCUMULATED DEPRECIATION	ENDING BOOK VALUE

PLANT ASSET RECORD, No. _____   General Ledger Account No. _____

Description _____   General Ledger Account _____

Date Bought _____   Serial Number _____   Original Cost _____

Estimated Useful Life _____   Estimated Salvage Value _____   Depreciation _____

Disposed of: Discarded _____   Sold _____   Traded _____

Date _____   Disposal Amount _____

YEAR	ANNUAL DEPRECIATION EXPENSE	ACCUMULATED DEPRECIATION	ENDING BOOK VALUE

8-12 CHALLENGE PROBLEM, p. 247

Recording entries for plant assets

GENERAL JOURNAL PAGE 7

DATE	ACCOUNT TITLE	DOC. NO.	POST. REF.	DEBIT	CREDIT

Name _____ Date _____ Class _____

8-12 CHALLENGE PROBLEM (concluded)

CASH PAYMENTS JOURNAL PAGE 12

	DATE	ACCOUNT TITLE	CK. NO.	POST. REF.	GENERAL DEBIT	GENERAL CREDIT	ACCOUNTS PAYABLE DEBIT	PURCHASES DISCOUNT CREDIT	CASH CREDIT	
1										1
2										2
3										3
4										4
5										5
6										6
7										7
8										8
9										9
10										10
11										11
12										12
13										13
14										14
15										15
16										16
17										17
18										18
19										19
20										20
21										21
22										22
23										23
24										24
25										25
26										26
27										27
28										28
29										29
30										30
31										31
32										32

Working Papers

COPYRIGHT © SOUTH-WESTERN EDUCATIONAL PUBLISHING

9-1 WORK TOGETHER, p. 255

Journalizing notes payable transactions

[4] CASH RECEIPTS JOURNAL — PAGE 15 (blank form with columns: Date, Account Title, Doc. No., Post. Ref., General Debit, General Credit, Accounts Receivable Credit, Sales Credit, Sales Tax Payable Debit, Sales Tax Payable Credit, Sales Discount Debit, Cash Debit)

[6] CASH PAYMENTS JOURNAL — PAGE 18 (blank form with columns: Date, Account Title, Ck. No., Post. Ref., General Debit, General Credit, Accounts Payable Debit, Purchases Discount Credit, Cash Credit)

Chapter 9 Accounting for Notes Payable, Prepaid Expenses, and Accrued Expenses • 317

9-1 WORK TOGETHER (concluded)

[5]

Maturity dates:

[5]

Interest due at maturity:

    Note signed May 14:

    Note signed June 5:

9-1 ON YOUR OWN, p. 255

Journalizing notes payable transactions

[7] CASH RECEIPTS JOURNAL PAGE 6

[9] CASH PAYMENTS JOURNAL PAGE 14

9-1 ON YOUR OWN (concluded)

[8]

Maturity dates:

[8]

Interest due at maturity:

    Note signed March 23:

    Note signed July 12:

9-2 WORK TOGETHER, p. 261

Journalizing adjusting and reversing entries for prepaid expenses initially recorded as expenses [4]

GENERAL JOURNAL
PAGE 15

DATE	ACCOUNT TITLE	DOC. NO.	POST. REF.	DEBIT	CREDIT

9-2 WORK TOGETHER (concluded)

[5]

GENERAL JOURNAL
PAGE 16

DATE	ACCOUNT TITLE	DOC. NO.	POST. REF.	DEBIT	CREDIT

9-2 ON YOUR OWN, p. 261

Journalizing adjusting and reversing entries for prepaid expenses initially recorded as expenses [6]

GENERAL JOURNAL — PAGE 13

DATE	ACCOUNT TITLE	DOC. NO.	POST. REF.	DEBIT	CREDIT

9-2 ON YOUR OWN (concluded)

[7]

GENERAL JOURNAL
PAGE 14

DATE	ACCOUNT TITLE	DOC. NO.	POST. REF.	DEBIT	CREDIT

9-3 WORK TOGETHER, p. 268

Journalizing adjusting and reversing entries for accrued expenses

a. One note payable is outstanding on December 31: 180-day, 12% note with First National Bank, $10,000, dated October 15.

b. Payroll information from the December 31 payroll:

Payroll and Employee Payroll Taxes		Employer Payroll Taxes	
Salaries—administrative	$1,200.00	Social Security tax	$143.00
Salaries—sales	1,000.00	Medicare tax	33.00
Federal income tax withheld	340.00	Federal unemployment tax	17.60
Social Security tax	143.00	State unemployment tax	118.80
Medicare tax	33.00		

c. Estimated federal income tax quarterly payment, $1,500.00.

[4]

GENERAL JOURNAL PAGE 13

DATE	ACCOUNT TITLE	DOC. NO.	POST. REF.	DEBIT	CREDIT

9-3 WORK TOGETHER (concluded)

[5]

GENERAL JOURNAL   PAGE 14

DATE	ACCOUNT TITLE	DOC. NO.	POST. REF.	DEBIT	CREDIT

9-3 ON YOUR OWN, p. 268

Journalizing adjusting and reversing entries for accrued expenses

a. One note payable is outstanding on December 31: 90-day, 10% note with American National Bank, $20,000, dated November 29.

b. Payroll information from the December 31 payroll:

Payroll and Employee Payroll Taxes		Employer Payroll Taxes	
Salaries—administrative	$1,500.00	Social Security tax	$214.50
Salaries—sales	1,800.00	Medicare tax	49.50
Federal income tax withheld	740.00	Federal unemployment tax	9.60
Social Security tax	214.50	State unemployment tax	64.80
Medicare tax	49.50		

c. Estimated federal income tax quarterly payment, $1,500.00.

[6]

GENERAL JOURNAL PAGE 13

DATE	ACCOUNT TITLE	DOC. NO.	POST. REF.	DEBIT	CREDIT

9-3 ON YOUR OWN (concluded)

[7]

GENERAL JOURNAL
PAGE 14

	DATE	ACCOUNT TITLE	DOC. NO.	POST. REF.	DEBIT	CREDIT	
1							1
2							2
3							3
4							4
5							5
6							6
7							7
8							8
9							9
10							10
11							11
12							12
13							13
14							14
15							15
16							16
17							17
18							18
19							19
20							20
21							21
22							22
23							23
24							24
25							25
26							26
27							27
28							28
29							29
30							30
31							31

9-1 APPLICATION PROBLEM, p. 270

Journalizing notes payable transactions

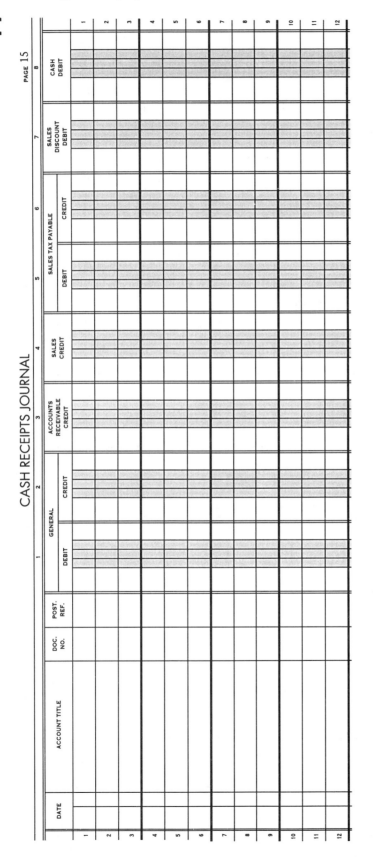

9-1 APPLICATION PROBLEM (concluded)

[2]

Maturity dates:

[3]

Interest due at maturity:

9-2 APPLICATION PROBLEM, p. 270

Journalizing adjusting and reversing entries for prepaid expenses initially recorded as expenses [1]

GENERAL JOURNAL

PAGE 13

DATE	ACCOUNT TITLE	DOC. NO.	POST. REF.	DEBIT	CREDIT

9-2 APPLICATION PROBLEM (concluded)

[2]

GENERAL JOURNAL

PAGE 1

	DATE	ACCOUNT TITLE	DOC. NO.	POST. REF.	DEBIT	CREDIT	
1							1
2							2
3							3
4							4
5							5
6							6
7							7
8							8
9							9
10							10
11							11
12							12
13							13
14							14
15							15
16							16
17							17
18							18
19							19
20							20
21							21
22							22
23							23
24							24
25							25
26							26
27							27
28							28
29							29
30							30
31							31

9-3 APPLICATION PROBLEM, p. 271

Journalizing adjusting and reversing entries for accrued expenses [1]

GENERAL JOURNAL

PAGE 13

DATE	ACCOUNT TITLE	DOC. NO.	POST. REF.	DEBIT	CREDIT

9-3 APPLICATION PROBLEM (concluded)

[2]

GENERAL JOURNAL

PAGE 1

DATE	ACCOUNT TITLE	DOC. NO.	POST. REF.	DEBIT	CREDIT

9-4 MASTERY PROBLEM, p. 271

Journalizing adjusting and reversing entries for prepaid expenses initially recorded as expenses and for accrued expenses [1]

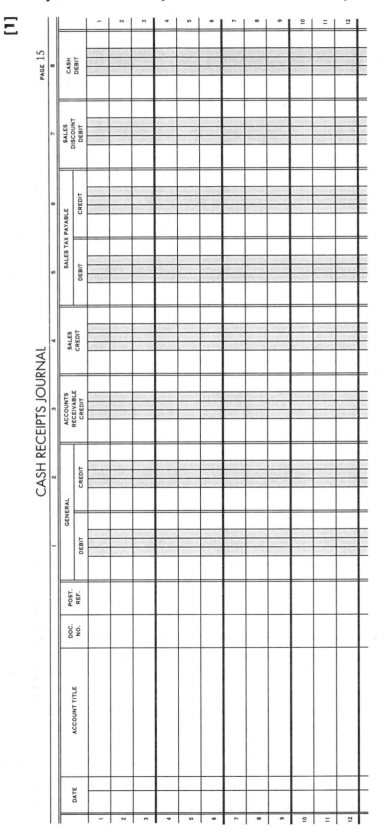

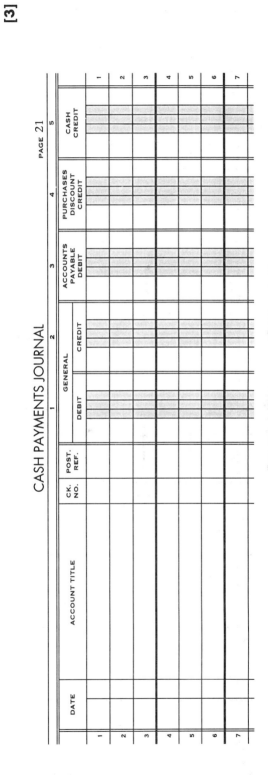

Chapter 9 Accounting for Notes Payable, Prepaid Expenses, and Accrued Expenses • 335

9-4 MASTERY PROBLEM (continued)

[2]

Maturity dates:

9-4 MASTERY PROBLEM (continued)

[4]

GENERAL JOURNAL PAGE 13

	DATE	ACCOUNT TITLE	DOC. NO.	POST. REF.	DEBIT	CREDIT	
1							1
2							2
3							3
4							4
5							5
6							6
7							7
8							8
9							9
10							10
11							11
12							12
13							13
14							14
15							15
16							16
17							17
18							18
19							19
20							20
21							21
22							22
23							23
24							24
25							25
26							26
27							27
28							28
29							29
30							30
31							31

9-4 MASTERY PROBLEM (concluded)

[5]

GENERAL JOURNAL

PAGE 1

	DATE	ACCOUNT TITLE	DOC. NO.	POST. REF.	DEBIT	CREDIT	
1							1
2							2
3							3
4							4
5							5
6							6
7							7
8							8
9							9
10							10
11							11
12							12
13							13
14							14
15							15
16							16
17							17
18							18
19							19
20							20
21							21
22							22
23							23
24							24
25							25
26							26
27							27
28							28
29							29
30							30
31							31

9-5 CHALLENGE PROBLEM, p. 272

Journalizing entries for notes payable and prepaid insurance when no reversing entries are recorded [1]

Cash		Income Summary

Accrued Interest		Interest Expense

Notes Payable		Retained Earnings

[1]

GENERAL JOURNAL
PAGE 13

	DATE	ACCOUNT TITLE	DOC. NO.	POST. REF.	DEBIT	CREDIT	
1							1
2							2
3							3
4							4
5							5
6							6
7							7
8							8
9							9
10							10
11							11

9-5 CHALLENGE PROBLEM (continued)

CASH RECEIPTS JOURNAL PAGE 11

DATE	ACCOUNT TITLE	DOC. NO.	POST. REF.	GENERAL DEBIT	GENERAL CREDIT	ACCOUNTS RECEIVABLE CREDIT	SALES CREDIT	SALES TAX PAYABLE DEBIT	SALES TAX PAYABLE CREDIT	SALES DISCOUNT DEBIT	CASH DEBIT

CASH PAYMENTS JOURNAL PAGE 4

DATE	ACCOUNT TITLE	CK. NO.	POST. REF.	GENERAL DEBIT	GENERAL CREDIT	ACCOUNTS PAYABLE DEBIT	PURCHASES DISCOUNT CREDIT	CASH CREDIT

9-5 CHALLENGE PROBLEM (continued)

[2]

Cash	Income Summary
Accrued Interest	Interest Expense
Notes Payable	Retained Earnings

[2]

GENERAL JOURNAL
PAGE 13

	DATE	ACCOUNT TITLE	DOC. NO.	POST. REF.	DEBIT	CREDIT	
1							1
2							2
3							3
4							4
5							5
6							6
7							7
8							8
9							9
10							10
11							11

9-5 CHALLENGE PROBLEM (concluded)

[2]

CASH RECEIPTS JOURNAL PAGE 11

DATE	ACCOUNT TITLE	DOC. NO.	POST. REF.	GENERAL DEBIT	GENERAL CREDIT	ACCOUNTS RECEIVABLE CREDIT	SALES CREDIT	SALES TAX PAYABLE DEBIT	SALES TAX PAYABLE CREDIT	SALES DISCOUNT DEBIT	CASH DEBIT

[2]

CASH PAYMENTS JOURNAL PAGE 4

DATE	ACCOUNT TITLE	CK. NO.	POST. REF.	GENERAL DEBIT	GENERAL CREDIT	ACCOUNTS PAYABLE DEBIT	PURCHASES DISCOUNT CREDIT	CASH CREDIT

10-1 WORK TOGETHER, p. 282

Journalizing notes receivable transactions [4]

GENERAL JOURNAL
PAGE 5

	DATE	ACCOUNT TITLE	DOC. NO.	POST. REF.	DEBIT	CREDIT	
1							1
2							2
3							3
4							4
5							5
6							6
7							7
8							8
9							9
10							10
11							11
12							12
13							13
14							14
15							15
16							16
17							17
18							18
19							19
20							20
21							21
22							22
23							23
24							24
25							25
26							26
27							27
28							28
29							29
30							30
31							31

10-1 WORK TOGETHER (concluded)

[4]

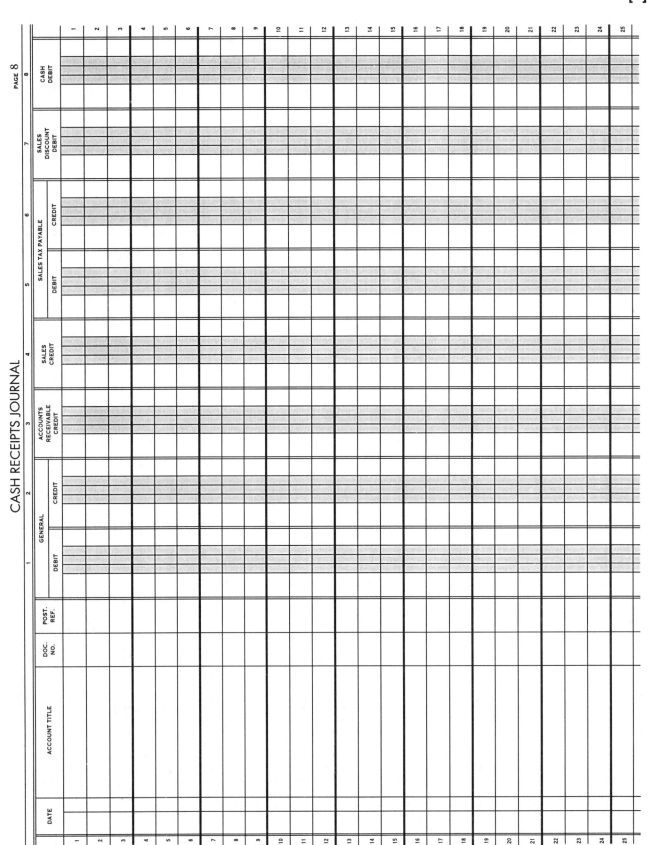

10-1 ON YOUR OWN, p. 282

Journalizing notes receivable transactions [5]

GENERAL JOURNAL

PAGE 6

DATE	ACCOUNT TITLE	DOC. NO.	POST. REF.	DEBIT	CREDIT

10-1 ON YOUR OWN (concluded)

[5]

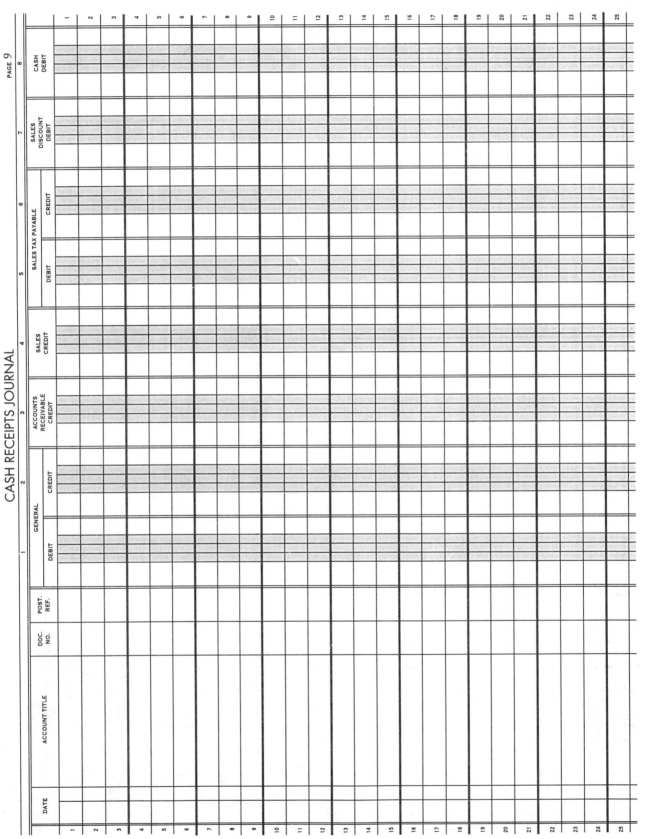

10-2 WORK TOGETHER, p. 287

Journalizing adjusting and reversing entries for unearned revenue initially recorded as revenue and for accrued revenue [6, 8]

GENERAL JOURNAL

PAGE 13

DATE	ACCOUNT TITLE	DOC. NO.	POST. REF.	DEBIT	CREDIT

10-2 WORK TOGETHER (concluded)

[7, 9]

GENERAL JOURNAL

PAGE 14

	DATE	ACCOUNT TITLE	DOC. NO.	POST. REF.	DEBIT	CREDIT	
1							1
2							2
3							3
4							4
5							5
6							6
7							7
8							8
9							9
10							10
11							11
12							12

Space for calculations:

10-2 ON YOUR OWN, p. 288

Journalizing adjusting and reversing entries for unearned revenue initially recorded as revenue and for accrued revenue [10, 12]

GENERAL JOURNAL — PAGE 19

DATE	ACCOUNT TITLE	DOC. NO.	POST. REF.	DEBIT	CREDIT

10-2 ON YOUR OWN (concluded)

[11, 13]

GENERAL JOURNAL PAGE 20

#	DATE	ACCOUNT TITLE	DOC. NO.	POST. REF.	DEBIT	CREDIT	
1							1
2							2
3							3
4							4
5							5
6							6
7							7
8							8
9							9
10							10
11							11
12							12

Space for calculations:

EXPLORE ACCOUNTING, p. 289

Projection assuming no factoring

Transaction	Week	Cash	Accounts Receivable	Inventory	Sales	Cost of Goods Sold
Balance	1			10,000		
Sales			2,000	(1,000)	2,000	1,000
Collection						
Purchases						
Balance	2	0	2,000	9,000	2,000	1,000
Sales						
Collection						
Purchases						
Balance	3					
Sales						
Collection						
Purchases						
Balance	4					
Sales						
Collection						
Purchases						
Balance	5					
Sales						
Collection						
Purchases						
Balance	6					
Sales						
Collection						
Purchases						
Balance	7					
Sales						
Collection						
Purchases						
Balance	8					
Sales						
Collection						
Purchases						
Balance	9					

Sales
Cost of Goods Sold

Income

Name _____ Date _____ Class _____

 EXPLORE ACCOUNTING (concluded)

Projection assuming factoring

Transaction	Week	Cash	Accounts Receivable	Inventory	Sales	Cost of Goods Sold	Factoring Expense
Balance	1			(10,000)			
Sales			2,000	(1,000)	2,000	1,000	
Collection							
Factoring		1,800					200
Purchases		(1,000)		1,000			
Balance	2	800	2,000	10,000	2,000	1,000	200
Sales							
Collection							
Factoring							
Purchases							
Balance	3						
Sales							
Collection							
Factoring							
Purchases							
Balance	4						
Sales							
Collection							
Factoring							
Purchases							
Balance	5						
Sales							
Collection							
Factoring							
Purchases							
Balance	6						
Sales							
Collection							
Factoring							
Purchases							
Balance	7						
Sales							
Collection							
Factoring							
Purchases							
Balance	8						
Sales							
Collection							
Factoring							
Purchases							
Balance	9						

Sales
Cost of Goods Sold
Factoring Expense

Income

Consultant's recommendation:

10-1 APPLICATION PROBLEM, p. 290

Journalizing transactions for notes receivable

GENERAL JOURNAL

PAGE 8

DATE	ACCOUNT TITLE	DOC. NO.	POST. REF.	DEBIT	CREDIT

10-1 APPLICATION PROBLEM (concluded)

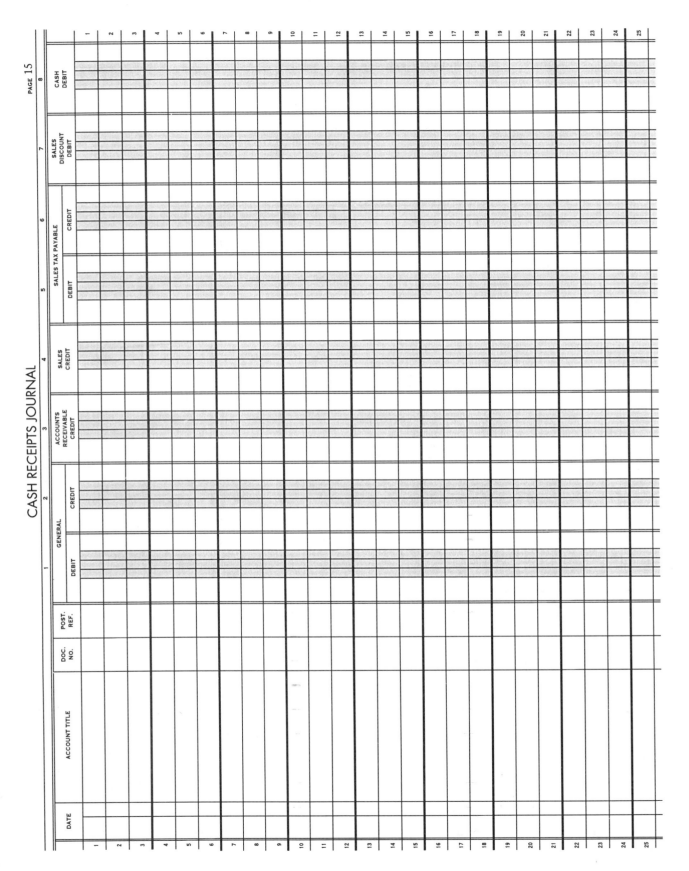

10-2 APPLICATION PROBLEM, p. 290

Journalizing adjusting and reversing entries for unearned revenue initially recorded as revenue [1]

GENERAL JOURNAL
PAGE 13

DATE	ACCOUNT TITLE	DOC. NO.	POST. REF.	DEBIT	CREDIT

10-2 APPLICATION PROBLEM (concluded)

[2]

GENERAL JOURNAL

PAGE 1

	DATE	ACCOUNT TITLE	DOC. NO.	POST. REF.	DEBIT	CREDIT	
1							1
2							2
3							3
4							4
5							5
6							6
7							7
8							8
9							9
10							10
11							11
12							12
13							13
14							14
15							15
16							16
17							17
18							18
19							19
20							20
21							21
22							22
23							23
24							24
25							25
26							26
27							27
28							28
29							29
30							30
31							31

10-3 APPLICATION PROBLEM, p. 290

Journalizing adjusting and reversing entries for accrued revenue [2]

GENERAL JOURNAL
PAGE 13

	DATE	ACCOUNT TITLE	DOC. NO.	POST. REF.	DEBIT	CREDIT	
1							1
2							2
3							3
4							4
5							5
6							6
7							7
8							8
9							9
10							10
11							11
12							12

[1]

Space for calculations:

Note	Accrued Interest Income
1	
2	
Total	

10-3 APPLICATION PROBLEM (concluded)

[3]

GENERAL JOURNAL

PAGE 1

	DATE	ACCOUNT TITLE	DOC. NO.	POST. REF.	DEBIT	CREDIT	
1							1
2							2
3							3
4							4
5							5
6							6
7							7
8							8
9							9
10							10
11							11
12							12
13							13
14							14
15							15
16							16
17							17
18							18
19							19
20							20
21							21
22							22
23							23
24							24
25							25
26							26
27							27
28							28
29							29
30							30
31							31

10-4 MASTERY PROBLEM, p. 291

Journalizing notes receivable, unearned revenue, and accrued revenue initially recorded as revenue transactions [1, 2]

GENERAL JOURNAL   PAGE 7

DATE	ACCOUNT TITLE	DOC. NO.	POST. REF.	DEBIT	CREDIT

[3]

GENERAL JOURNAL   PAGE 1

DATE	ACCOUNT TITLE	DOC. NO.	POST. REF.	DEBIT	CREDIT

10-4 MASTERY PROBLEM (concluded)

[1]

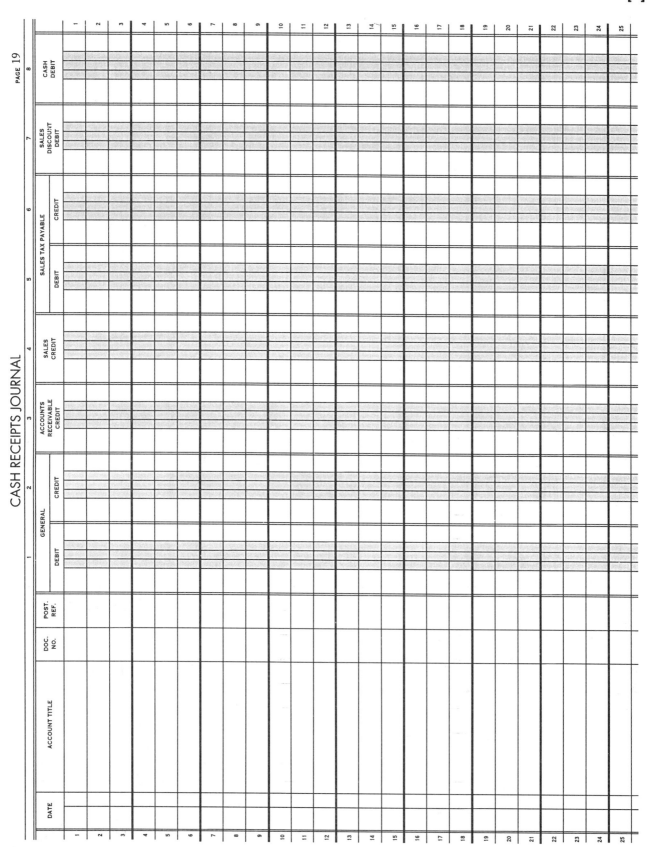

10-5 CHALLENGE PROBLEM, p. 291

Journalizing accounts and notes receivable

GENERAL JOURNAL PAGE 7

DATE	ACCOUNT TITLE	DOC. NO.	POST. REF.	DEBIT	CREDIT

10-5 CHALLENGE PROBLEM (concluded)

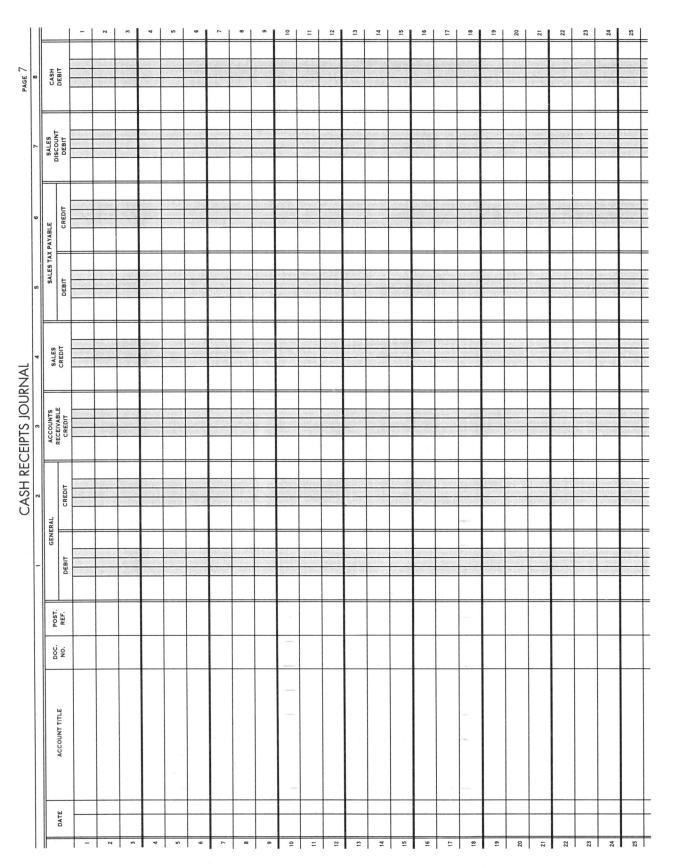

Name _____ Date _____ Class _____

Extra form

GENERAL JOURNAL

PAGE

	DATE	ACCOUNT TITLE	DOC. NO.	POST. REF.	DEBIT	CREDIT
1						
2						
3						
4						
5						
6						
7						
8						
9						
10						
11						
12						
13						
14						
15						
16						
17						
18						
19						
20						
21						
22						
23						
24						
25						
26						
27						
28						
29						
30						
31						

Extra form

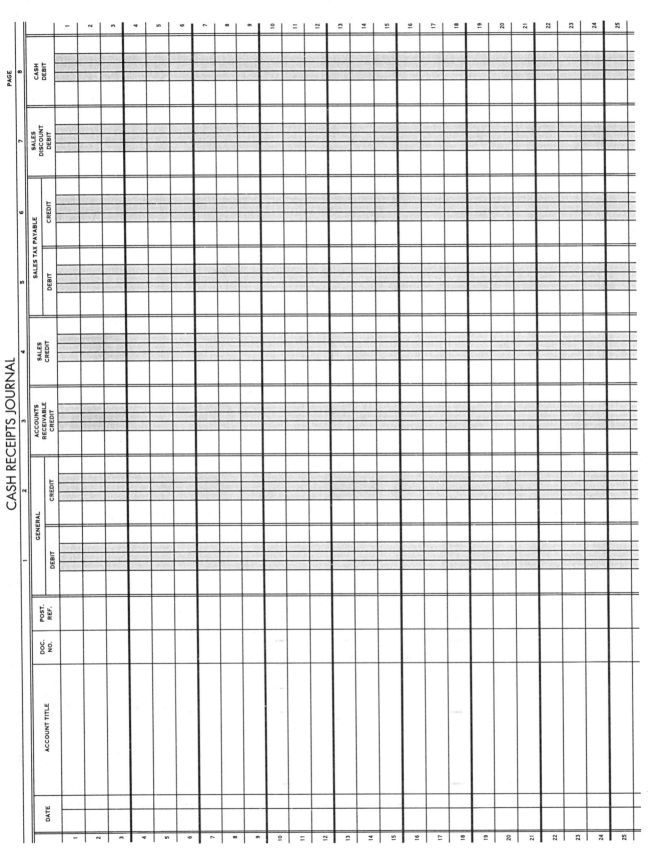

Extra form

CASH PAYMENTS JOURNAL

Extra form

Extra form

Extra form